Energy Efficiency in
OLD HOUSES

Energy Efficiency in
OLD HOUSES

Martin Godfrey Cook

THE CROWOOD PRESS

First published in 2009 by
The Crowood Press Ltd
Ramsbury, Marlborough
Wiltshire SN8 2HR

www.crowood.com

British Library Cataloguing-in-Publication Data
A catalogue record for this book is available from the British Library.

ISBN 978 1 84797 077 0

Disclaimer
The author and the publisher do not accept responsibility, or liability, in any
manner whatsoever for any error or omission, nor any loss, damage, injury,
or adverse outcome of any kind incurred as a result of the use of the
information contained in this book, or reliance upon it. Readers are advised to
seek professional energy efficiency advice relating to their particular property,
project and circumstances before embarking on any building or related work.

Typeset by Servis Filmsetting Ltd, Stockport, Cheshire
Printed and bound in Singapore by Craft Print International

Contents

Preface

We live in an increasingly uncertain world, with dwindling natural resources, rapidly expanding population growth and finite reserves of fossil fuels. Coal is the fossil fuel that we have the most of, but continued burning of coal without clean technology is dramatically increasing levels of carbon dioxide in the atmosphere to unprecedented levels. We are currently living in the midst of a giant chemistry experiment, and already experiencing the previously unimagined consequences of our actions. Many experts now claim that we have only five to fifteen years of 'business as usual' left until we reach the 'tipping point', after which we will have lost any further influence over the course that global warming and climate change takes.

These views are put forward by respected individuals and organizations, from the scientific and other communities. Most of them have studied this situation since at least the last energy crisis in the mid-seventies, when politics dictated dramatic rises in the price of oil in Western countries. All of them, such as the World Wildlife Fund, cite energy efficiency as one of the key strategic actions we must take now.

The last energy crisis stimulated government and individual action, legislation, research and innovation – we have been there before, and responded positively. Administrations such as the State of California, which continued to actively pursue an environmentally led agenda through legislation, incentives and other means, have kept their *per capita* energy consumption down to 1970s levels – while many other states in the USA, and other countries, have seen their energy consumption inexorably rise over the last three decades. The point is: we are capable of averting disaster. The question is: will we do so in time?

Politics, globalization and governments seem like abstractions to most of us, but there is something we can all do tomorrow – or even today …

Put our old houses in energy-efficient order …

Martin Godfrey Cook
Hertfordshire
May 2008

Introduction

OVERVIEW

A quarter of the houses in Britain were built a century or more ago, when the complexities of modern building legislation and energy performance certificates were still far into the unknown future. Britain has some of the oldest housing stock in the world, and even those old houses that are not listed or protected in conservation areas are invariably prized for their character and collective heritage value. Consequently, most people in Britain live in an old house, at least ten years old and more likely to be fifty or over a hundred years old. In the UK, 62 per cent of all dwellings were built before 1965, and 35 per cent were built before World War II. The most common dwelling type in England is the semi-detached house: 4.9 million, or 31 per cent of the total stock. Purpose-built low-rise flats and detached houses are the next most common property types.

It is unlikely that these houses are the most energy- or carbon-efficient dwellings, even though improvements such as added insulation, double glazing and modern boilers were made, particularly since the last oil shock of the mid-1970s. Compared with other Western European countries, such as Germany, Britain has the disadvantage, in energy efficiency terms, of more old housing stock. Paradoxically, this also presents us with an unparalleled opportunity: to upgrade our old houses to modern energy efficiency standards to save energy, money, and possibly ourselves in the face of global warming and climate change.

Houses that are decades old are likely to have undergone many changes in ownership, technology and adaptation to modern lifestyles. The fact that these dwellings are still in use proves their fundamental sustainability – and there is little reason why the vast majority of old houses should not continue to function efficiently for many more decades, or even centuries, to come. In some respects old houses were built more solidly than many modern dwellings, and the materials and workmanship that went into them represent a large investment of embodied energy and traditional building skills. The longevity of the old houses that are still with us proves that they were the best built, otherwise they would not have survived so long. Old house types such as Victorian terraces still represent a much emulated model of sustainable development and community, particularly in terms of planning density and their location near to town and city centres.

As we rely increasingly on finite fossil fuel reserves to drive our modern lifestyles, and as global population increases, we become inherently less and less sustainable as a species on this planet. The creation and supply of energy has detrimental effects on our environment, effects which impact on human health and the natural world around us, from air pollution created by burning fossil fuels and by radioactivity from nuclear power in the developed world, to the destruction of woodlands to supply fires for cooking and warmth in the developing world. We have finite resources of fossil fuels on the planet, and the burning of fuels such as coal results in increased carbon dioxide emissions, which are contributing to climate change and global warming.

About half of the energy we use is used in buildings, and half of that is used in our houses – and cost-effective improvements in the energy efficiency of our

Typical Victorian terraced housing.

old houses could reduce carbon dioxide emissions by at least a quarter immediately. Australia's recent banning of inefficient incandescent light bulbs by 2010, forcing a switch to compact fluorescent light bulbs (CFLs), highlights the potential power of the cumulative effect of individual actions. About 90 per cent of the energy used by incandescent bulbs is wasted, producing heat rather than light. At the beginning of 2008, retailers in the UK began a voluntary four-year scheme to stop selling inefficient light bulbs – the scheme aims to save 5 million tonnes of carbon dioxide emissions a year as people turn to low-energy light bulbs instead.

In the words of Australia's Environment Minister:

> ... if the whole world switched to these bulbs today, we would reduce our consumption of electricity by an amount equal to five times Australia's annual consumption of electricity.

GLOBAL WARMING AND CLIMATE CHANGE

In the UK we use several times the energy, individually, that our Edwardian forbears did just a century ago, and there are many more of us now. If it were not for the energy shocks of the 1970s, when the price of oil rose dramatically for political reasons, we would use much more than this in our domestic lives alone. The number of houses has more than tripled over the last century: between 1900 and 1998 the housing stock of Great Britain increased from about 7 million to 22 million permanent dwellings, and owner occupation of property has increased from 10 per cent of homes in 1914 to 68 per cent in 1999.

In this respect, the introduction of energy efficiency measures, such as increased roof insulation, from the 1970s onwards was successful. However, we now increasingly face the prospect of climate change,

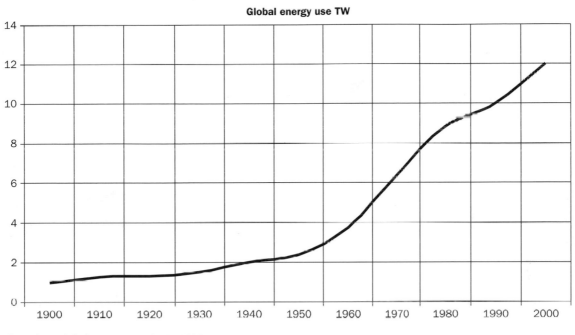

Growth in global energy use 1900–2000.

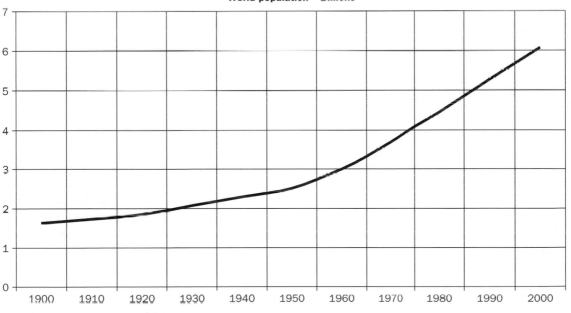

Growth in world population 1900–2000.

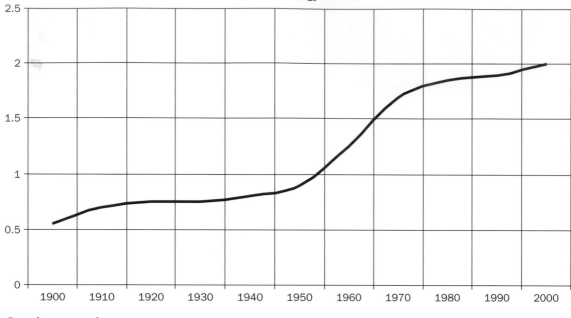

Personal energy use KW

Growth in personal energy use 1900–2000.

thought by many experts to be the most serious threat to the survival of humankind that we have ever faced. Some experts claim that we have about ten years before climate change becomes irreversible and there is nothing further we can do about it. It is only by decreasing our individual 'carbon footprint' that we can begin to avert global disasters – and our old homes are the most obvious place to start living as if we had one planet, rather than several. As well as giving us a clear conscience, adopting energy efficiency measures in our old houses will also save money, and the price of energy is unlikely to decrease. The introduction of energy certificates, rating energy usage from A to F in houses, should also make more energy-efficient dwellings more marketable.

Recent seminal reports, such as the Stern Report in the UK[1], and associated media attention, have raised awareness of the challenge of climate change to the extent that four out of five people in the UK are now concerned about climate change and global warming. (The average temperature in the UK in 2007 was 9.6°C, just below the record highest temperature of 9.7°C set in 2006. These are a full degree above the long-term average yearly temperature of 8.6°C.) The same majority now claims to have installed some energy-efficient light bulbs in their houses, and nine out of ten people in the UK also claim to switch off the lights when leaving a room.

Similar majorities of the UK population also:
- think that human activities contribute to global warming;
- think the seasons are not arriving at the same time of year as they used to;
- think the government should do more to tackle global warming;
- think that climate change will impact upon their children;
- believe they have personally seen evidence of climate change;
- believe that if no change is made, the world will experience a major eco-crisis soon.

It would appear that the general public are right in their concern about global warming and climate change. A Meteorological Office spokesman recently suggested that 2007 would be the second warmest year on record (the warmest was 2006) since records began in 1914. And he added, 'The warmest years all being in the last six suggests that climate change is happening and is affecting the UK.'[2]

Climate change brought about by man-made emissions of greenhouse gases is identified as the greatest challenge facing human society at the beginning of the twentieth-first century. The United Nations Intergovernmental Panel on Climate Change (IPCC) has suggested that human society could eventually be reduced to a few isolated groups eking out an existence near the poles. As implausible as this scenario sounds, we must all consider the consequences of not taking action to reduce the risk of this grim eventuality.

> We are currently in a twilight war against climate change; we have identified the enemy, we are marshalling our forces and we are skirmishing. But within fifteen years we will be in all-out war against climate change, and it will influence everything that we do.
>
> *Colin Challen, MP, Chair – All Party Parliamentary*
> *Climate Change Group*

A foretaste of civic disruption relating to energy supply was provided in the mid-seventies, when OAPEC (Organisation of Arab Petroleum Exporting Countries) member countries placed an embargo on oil exports to countries that had supported Israel in the Yom Kippur War (the United States, its Western European allies and Japan). This oil crisis began at the end of 1973, and oil prices nearly quadrupled over the next few years. Inflation in the UK reached 25 per cent by 1975, which combined with the 'coal crisis' and strikes to bring about the 'three day week' and 'stagflation' (rising unemployment with a rising rate of inflation).

A state of emergency was declared in the UK, which led to the use of emergency powers to enact legislation to prohibit and reduce the consumption of electricity for space heating in buildings used by the public – these included offices, showrooms, shops, banks, petrol stations, restaurants, bars, studios, public halls, schools, churches and places of recreation, entertainment or sport.

The Fuel and Electricity (Control) Bill became an Act on 6 December 1973, and gave the government the legislative basis that could have brought in petrol rationing as well as other powers over the energy supply industry. Legislation under the Act included the prohibition of heating public buildings to a temperature above 63°F (17.25°C); in 1974 this was increased to 66.2°F (19°C), and remains on the statute book, recently being subsumed into European Union legislation. According to Edward Heath's biographer:

> Behind the scenes . . . the Civil Contingencies Unit . . . prepared a complete emergency structure of regional government in the event of a large-scale breakdown of energy supplies. Across the country a network of regional commissioners was ready to maintain basic services, as in a nuclear alert.[3]

The oil shocks of the mid-seventies provided a much needed spur to improving energy efficiency and exploring alternative sources of energy as an economic and national necessity. But it also increased the West's dependence on coal and nuclear power – the former, obviously, a major source of carbon dioxide emissions, and the latter lauded by some as an immediate way of reducing carbon dioxide emissions to ameliorate global warming and climate change. James Lovelock, author of the controversial Gaia theory of the Earth, argues that nuclear power is preferable to the further burning of fossil fuels for energy production.

The Gaia Theory
The Gaia theory, named after the Greek Earth goddess, proposes that the planet is a complex, holistic and inter-related system – akin to a living organism. The theory holds that all living things affect the life-sustaining qualities of the Earth's environment, and provide feedback for it to remain in equilibrium. The theory started as an ecological hypothesis when Lovelock was working independently for NASA in the 1960s, on the means of detecting life on Mars.

Although recent events have focused the likelihood of future national states of emergency emerging in response to major terrorist incidents, major natural and environmental disasters such as serious flooding are also causing increasing alarm.

New houses add only about 1 or 2 per cent to the housing stock each year, so it follows that it is in the existing housing stock that energy efficiency improvements have to be made to combat climate change. Most people in the UK are responsible for about 10 tonnes of greenhouse gas emissions each year: achieving a sustainable level of greenhouse gas emissions involves reducing our emissions to about 2 tonnes each per year. Fortunately there are invariably cost-effective and relatively easy ways of doing this, by upgrading our old houses while saving money on energy bills and making our properties worth more, and more marketable at the same time. Our war against climate change must begin on the home front, and usually with some very mundane but highly effective actions, such as improving insulation, preventing heat loss through draughts, and installing modern lighting and heating technology and controls.

ENERGY EFFICIENCY PRINCIPLES FOR OLD HOUSES

Much political mileage was attempted recently from small-scale domestic renewable energy interventions such as photovoltaic solar panels and wind turbines on domestic roofs. However, the latter vary widely in effectiveness due to low wind speeds in most urban and suburban areas, while the former are still very expensive and have a typical payback period of several decades. Such interventions are symbolically dramatic, but many energy conservation solutions are simpler, cheaper and generally easier to install, maintain and operate. They are also well tried and tested solutions that have been around since at least the last oil shocks thirty years ago. Indeed, many energy efficiency improvements in old houses become marginal investments when combined with necessary or planned maintenance and refurbishment work. However, it is important to take an integrated design approach to ensure that improved insulation, heating and ventilation are working together properly and optimally.

Insulation

Insulation will slow down the rate of heat lost from an old house so that less heat is required to maintain the same internal temperature. Although heat rises, most heat is probably lost through the walls of old houses, as they are usually a much larger surface area of the house than the roof. If windows are single glazed, clearly a great deal of heat will be lost through them – about three or four times the amount of heat lost through a double-glazed window of the same size, and about six times the heat lost through a triple-glazed window. About a quarter of all the energy we use to heat our homes escapes through single-glazed windows.

A typical single-glazed window has a U-value of about 4 or 5 watts per square meter, compared to that of double glazing at about 1.5, and triple glazing at about 0.5. U-value is a measure of the thermal conductivity of elements of a building, such as the window, wall, floor and roof. A typical 9in (215mm) thick solid brick wall has a U-value of 2.5 watts per square meter – which means that 2.5 watts of energy are lost through a square metre of it in one hour.

However, the easiest and cheapest insulation improvement to an old house is invariably to insulate the loft space – after that it is important to minimize overall heat loss, and to avoid thermal or cold bridges that can lead to condensation problems.

Condensation

Condensation occurs when warm air meets a cold surface, and the moisture in the air condenses on the surface, such as the cold face of a single-glazed window. Most old, traditionally constructed houses are draughty, some almost deliberately so in order that moisture from rainfall soaking into solid walls, and from other sources, is ventilated to the outside. Modern house construction techniques rely on impervious layers, such as damp-proof courses (DPC) and damp-proof membranes (DPM) to exclude moisture from the outside. Old houses still need to 'breathe' when their insulation and air-tightness is improved, or problems of condensation will occur. Even in modern house construction timber roof structure spaces are ventilated, or 'breather membranes' are installed, to

Condensation on the inside of a window.

prevent moisture build-up from condensation damaging the building fabric, such as structural timbers.

The inappropriate application of modern construction techniques to old houses frequently causes condensation and other problems – such as the use of Portland cement instead of lime mortar, and the inadvertent blocking of ventilation grilles to roof spaces, or suspended timber floor spaces, when installing insulation or making other improvements. Controlled ventilation is required in any house, as moisture will always be created from the occupants and particularly in kitchens and bathrooms. Improvements to old houses should not completely exclude ventilation, unless systems such as mechanical ventilation with heat recovery are adopted.

Heating

Heating has evolved from a luxury into something of a necessity for many people. Historically, people wore more layers of heavy clothing than we do these days, indoors and outside. We have come to expect comfort in our shirt sleeves in our houses, and even in other building types. Even as recently as 1970, the average UK house was heated to a temperature of only 54°F (12°C) – this had risen to 64°F (18°C) by 2003, and is probably in the seventies F (twenties C) by now. The government of the day passed legislation in the 1970s to limit the temperatures in public buildings to 64–66°F (18–19°C) to save energy as a result of the last oil shock. (This was the Control of Fuel and Electricity Act, 1973, and subsequent Orders. The 1980 Heating Control Order requires that 'No person shall use, cause and/or permit the use of electricity or fuel for the purpose of heating premises so as to cause the temperature of those premises to exceed 19 degrees Celsius, which is equivalent to 66.2 degrees Fahrenheit.')

This caused much consternation in public sector offices where it was often actually enforced – but it should be a comfortable enough temperature, with your thermal underwear on, at least. Wear a sweater and turn the thermostat down by 2°F (1°C) to save 10 per cent of your heating energy, and reduce carbon dioxide emissions!

13

Heating systems that are oversized are likely to waste energy. Insulation improvements to old houses will reduce the amount of heat needed, making it a good time to upgrade your heating system and controls to reap further efficiencies and savings.

Ventilation

Ventilation is traditionally a problem in old houses, due to uncontrolled air infiltration and heat escaping through gaps around doors, windows and other openings. Even the general building fabric is sometimes 'leaky' in older forms of construction, such as timber-framed weatherboarding. An air-pressure test is sometimes necessary to determine exactly where draughts are originating from – this can help to target improvements in the right areas, and ensure that investments are cost effective.

Ventilation is ideally controlled by occupants through trickle vents in windows and extract fans (often with heat recovery), rather than uncontrolled through undraught-stripped windows, doors and other gaps. Effective draught-stripping is generally one of the first energy efficiency measures to implement in an old house. However, old houses require

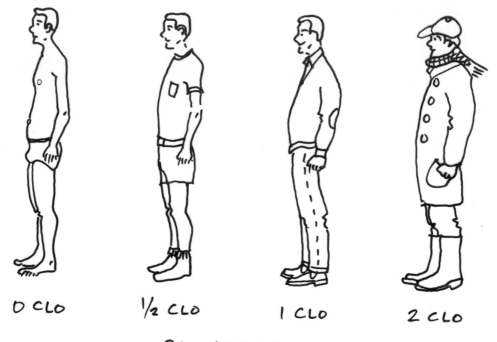

Clo value	Clothing	Average comfort level in degrees Centigrade			
		Strolling	Standing	Sitting	Sleeping
0	Nude	21	27	28	30
0.5	Light clothing	15	23	25	27
1	Normal clothing	8	19	21	24
1.5	Heavy clothing	0	14	18	21
2	Very heavy clothing		10	14	18

The thermal effect of clothing and activity.

IMPROVEMENT / OPPORTUNITY	Internal wall insulation	Double-glazing	Cavity wall insulation	External wall insulation	Extract ventilation	Draught stripping	Trickle ventilation	Insulate loft	Insulate water pipes	Ventilate loft space	Insulate floors	Add porch or vestibule	Low-energy lighting	Insulate hot water cylinder	Improve controls	Fit replacement combi boiler
Moving into an existing house	X	X	X	X	X	X	X	X	X	X	X	X	X	X	X	X
Loft conversion						X	X	X	X	X	X		X			
Refitting kitchens & bathrooms	X	X			X	X								X	X	X
Adding a conservatory	X	X	X	X	X	X	X					X	X		X	
Repointing of walls			X													
Repairing frost-damaged walls or render/upgrading external appearance				X												
Replastering	X															
Replacing wall ties			X													
Rewiring	X								X				X		X	
Replacement windows		X				X	X									
Repairing cladding				X												
Re-roofing/roof repairs						X		X	X	X						
Replacing external doors						X						X				
Repairing ground floors						X			X		X					
Heating and plumbing repairs									X					X	X	X
Increase security		X				X							X			

Opportunities for including energy efficiency measures into repair and improvement work.

adequate ventilation to allow moisture from traditional construction such as rain-soaked solid walls and roof voids to evaporate and dry out. A ventilation strategy should always include energy-efficient and controlled ways to ensure adequate ventilation in traditional buildings.

ENERGY PERFORMANCE CERTIFICATES

The introduction of home information packs (HIPs) into the UK housing market, prepared by house vendors for the information of potential buyers, proved controversial throughout 2007. However, in early 2008 energy performance certificates (EPCs) were required on the transaction of all dwellings, and it seems likely that the requirement will extend to commercial buildings throughout 2008. This legislation stems from the European Union Energy Performance of Buildings Directive, 2002.

The concept of rating the energy efficiency of housing and other buildings on an A–G rating scale comes from the familiar colour-code scales that were introduced for white goods, such as washing machines and refrigerators, some years ago. These enabled consumers to make informed decisions about the energy efficiency of goods they were buying. The colour-coded rating system extends from a green A-rating, which indicates a house that is very energy efficient with potentially lower running costs, to a red G-rated house that is not energy efficient and generally has higher running costs.

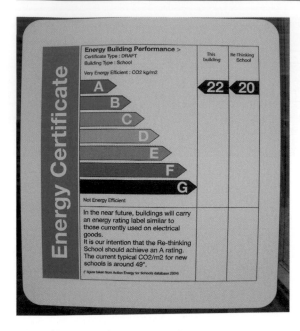

Typical energy performance certificate.

for improvement in the ageing housing stock, and most of it is in private ownership.

CONCLUSIONS

The continued occupation of old houses, combined with performance improvement measures, is the most energy-efficient form of property development. In fact, the best and most economical time to improve energy efficiency is in the context of refurbishment, extension, restoration or conservation of existing houses. Old houses contain embodied energy from the labour and material invested in them when they were constructed, and to demolish them is a waste of energy and finite resources. However, a particular challenge with old houses is to upgrade their fabric and performance sympathetically – a typical dilemma, for example, is the appearance of windows.

Recent estimates suggest that in order to reduce carbon dioxide emissions by 60 per cent by 2050, in line with international governmental agreements such as the Kyoto Protocol, nearly half-a-million existing dwellings would have to be refurbished each year in the UK. The English House Condition Survey shows that the age of a house more often than not dictates its energy performance: thus dwellings built before 1919 have an average SAP rating of thirty-nine, while those built after 1990 have an average SAP rating of sixty-five. Case studies suggest that simple packages of measures can cost effectively improve the energy and environmental performance of typical Victorian terraces and later semi-detached houses to modern standards.

The intention is also to show the environmental rating of houses, by way of a corresponding carbon dioxide emissions rating, again on a scale of A to G. An A-rated house is potentially very environmentally friendly with lower carbon dioxide emissions, while a G-rated house is generally not environmentally friendly and has higher carbon dioxide emissions. The ultimate intention of the legislation is to improve the energy performance of houses by allowing house buyers to make informed decisions about their purchase. To this end the certificate shows a current rating as well as a potential rating, and gives some generic advice and recommendations to improve the home's energy performance.

A useful analogy is probably that of an MOT for a car – no doubt everyone whinged when these were first introduced in the 1960s, but now they are taken for granted and inform our purchasing decisions. Similar to the later addition of emissions testing as part of an automobile's MOT, the framework of the house EPC provides an opportunity to add other performance information – such as water consumption, for example. It seems likely that future such legislation will be performance based, as we seek to increase environmental sustainability – and there is certainly scope

Over a third of the UK housing stock was built before 1940, and two-thirds before 1965, largely as a result of post-war reconstruction. The most common house is the semi-detached (5 million – 30 per cent of stock), followed by purpose-built low-rise flats and detached houses. The rate of owner occupation has increased from 10 per cent in 1914 to 71 per cent in 2007. Roughly half of the UK construction industry expenditure relates to the repair, refurbishment and maintenance of the existing building stock. New building stock only adds about 1 per cent to the stock each year. Old houses are where energy efficiency and environmental improvements have to be made to combat climate change and global warming, and to reduce potentially increasing energy costs.

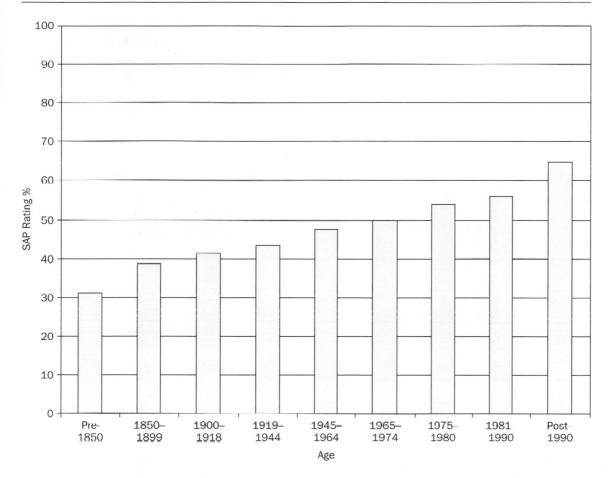

Energy performance of housing stock in England.

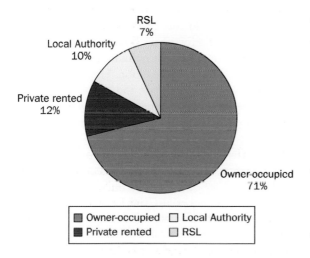

Ownership of UK housing stock.

SUMMARY

- Most people in the United Kingdom live in an old house, at least ten years old and more likely to be fifty or over a hundred years old. The housing stock in the UK is the oldest in the developed world – a third was built before World War II. The most common dwelling type in England is the semi-detached house, which makes up about a third of the housing stock.

- As we rely increasingly on finite fossil fuel reserves to drive our modern lifestyles, and as global population increases, we become inherently less and less sustainable as a species on this planet.

- About half of the energy we use is used in buildings, and half of that in our houses – cost-effective improvements in the energy efficiency of our old

17

Typical old house refurbishment dilemma – window appearance.

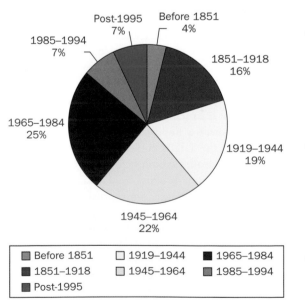

Age of the housing stock in England.

houses could reduce carbon dioxide emissions by at least a quarter immediately.

- In the UK we use several times the energy, individually, than our Edwardian forbearers did just a century ago, and there are many more of us now. If it were not for the energy shocks of the 1970s, when the price of oil rose dramatically, we would be using much more than this in our domestic lives alone.

- We now increasingly face the prospect of climate change – thought by many experts to be the most serious threat to the survival of humankind that we have ever faced. Some experts claim that we have about ten years before climate change becomes irreversible, and there is nothing further we can do about it.

- Although recent events have focused the likelihood of future national states of emergency emerging in response to major terrorist incidents, major natural and environmental disasters such as serious flooding are also causing increasing alarm.

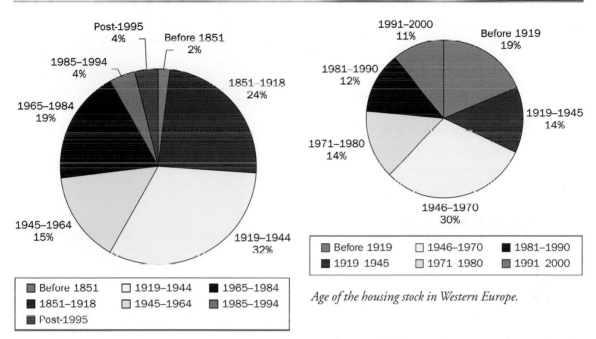

Age of the housing stock in London.

Age of the housing stock in Western Europe.

- Our war against climate change must begin on the home front, and usually with some very mundane but highly effective actions, such as improving insulation, preventing heat loss through draughts, and installing modern lighting and heating technology and controls.
- There are well tried and tested energy efficiency improvements to old houses, which become marginal investments when combined with necessary or planned maintenance and refurbishment work. However, it is important to take an integrated design approach, to ensure that improved insulation, heating and ventilation are working together properly and optimally.

- The crucial difference between modern and traditional construction is that modern houses use impervious modern materials such as cement and plastic to keep water out, while traditional houses were made of materials such as solid brickwork, stone, timber and lime – these materials absorb moisture and then dry out with sufficient ventilation.
- In 2008 energy performance certificates (EPCs) were required on the transaction of all dwellings. The colour-coded rating system extends from a green A-rating, which indicates a house that is very energy efficient with lower running costs, to a red G-rated house that is not energy efficient and has higher running costs.

CHAPTER 1

The Historic Development of Houses

THE FIRST MILLENNIUM: ROMAN TO ANGLO-SAXON

At some stage in our past, such as in the Garden of Eden in Paradise, it may have been warm enough for us not to need shelter – or even clothes, for that matter! However, we now appear to have drifted a long way away from such ideal conditions, not mentioning the effects of climate change. But in our dim and distant past the primary concern in ancient times was undoubtedly trying to keep warm in the wintry north of countries such as Britain. Sheltering in primitive huts and surrounded by forests, there was plenty of fuel for fires, and the odd drop of rain from the hole in the centre of the hut to allow the smoke to escape, was a small price to pay for warmth, which meant survival.

A thousand years ago when Britain was a wild frontier on the edge of the Roman Empire, our imperial rulers obviously also considered warmth in this northern outpost a primary concern. Archaeological evidence shows that most of the Roman villas scattered around the countryside had underfloor heating, or hypocausts. This ancient central heating must have consumed vast amounts of energy from the timber in the forests, not to mention its labour intensiveness. But that was of little concern to the Romans in a slave-based economy and surrounded by trees in Britain. However, the Romans can possibly lay claim to the first energy-efficient buildings at Bath, where they used geothermal heating.

Britain drifted into the Dark Ages when the Romans withdrew after the sack of Rome in 410AD. Little domestic archaeology remains from these times because most buildings were made of wood after the departure of the Romans. However, archaeological excavations show that the average Anglo-Saxon lived in an oval-shaped house, roofed over with large timbers interwoven with branches and smeared with clay: wattle and daub. The building materials of timber were all around, and the landscape was a reversed view from that of a train passing through the countryside today – about 90 per cent forest and 10 per cent open clearing. Naturally, timber as an energy source was also abundant, although inconvenient due to its smokiness and because it was hard work to cut and gather from the woodlands. The energy preoccupation for the majority of the population during these centuries was the provision of heat for cooking and space heating.

Timber-framed buildings were made reasonably comfortable, and with enough straw the thatched roof might even match the thermal properties of a modern roof. Even the infill of the timber framing, made of wattle, mud, straw and animal hair, might be built up enough to provide modest levels of thermal insulation. In many ways such a house might be more comfortable than a stone house, where tapestries were placed on the walls to take some of the chill away from cold stone walls. At least in the timber house the organic nature of the construction meant that it could be improved and repaired quite easily from materials to hand, and draught-stripping could be effected with animal hair or vegetable fibres.

Typical medieval timber-framed house.

THE NEXT HALF-MILLENIUM: NORMAN TO TUDOR

The development of the English house is indebted to the Normans and the stone buildings they created, first in the form of castles for defence. But the Normans' great architectural achievements were in the realm of stone churches and cathedrals rather than domestic architecture. Stone construction was developed by trial and error, and the towers of no fewer than eight of England's early cathedrals collapsed during, or not many years after, construction.

Massive stone constructions such as cathedrals and castles are wonderfully cool and comfortable in summer. The thick stone walls are able to absorb heat energy from the sun and store it, to give it out again during the cooler night – just when we need it. This thermal mass is less useful in winter, however, as it means that heat from the fire is also being absorbed by

stone walls, as well as heating the occupants. So we can imagine that the Normans' major concern was heating their stone buildings in winter, by burning wood from the now slowly diminishing forests around them.

In houses with thick stone walls, lighting would also be a concern and many of the internal rooms would be very gloomy, even by day. By night, those who could afford it would use beeswax candles, and the less well off would resort to poorer quality tallow. Timber floors and roofs could only span a limited distance, so narrow plans were lit and ventilated from both sides. But before the widespread availability of glass to make glazed windows, wood shutters were used, sliding or folding. Shutters clearly lacked the convenience of glass, because if they were shut the interior was dingy. The glass industry grew in Germany and Czechoslovakia in the Middle Ages, but glass did not become readily available for buildings that were not special ones until the seventeenth and eighteenth centuries. Before that time even quite important buildings might have had animal skins or waxed paper as makeshift glazing in their windows.

Most buildings, both houses and other types, were timber framed, and this form of construction, unlike early solid stone structures, at least allowed copious space for windows between the framing. However, stone masonry skills developed to the extent that there were less dramatic collapses of stone buildings, so much so that by about 1500, Perpendicular Gothic architecture could boast much smaller areas of stone walls and correspondingly larger window areas – the weight of the stone walls was supported by sophisticated buttresses, and flying buttresses in the case of churches and cathedrals. Houses developed as the growth of trade allowed rich merchants to build more elaborate dwellings, and others tried to emulate them. Houses were predominately made out of timber, but in deforested areas stone was a more readily available local building material. Local vernacular traditions of house building continued to develop, which displayed local craftsmanship and materials to best effect.

Medieval society was fairly static, and economic development was occasionally stunted by civil wars, until the Black Death dramatically changed society. The plague that swept through Europe and eventually Britain in the mid-fourteenth century killed about a third of the population, and in its wake there was such

a shortage of labour that the old manorial and tythe system was destroyed by the new market for money in exchange for labour, and a much more mobile labour force. Industries such as wool and cloth thrived and needed to be near water, effectively using hydro-power – as did agriculture, which also used wind power in mills to grind corn. There was also a mining industry that had to grapple with the problems of lighting and ventilating mining shafts. In addition, nascent manufacturing industries developed in small places such as Manchester and Birmingham, which complained that trade and progress were being hampered by the closed shops of the craft guilds in established market towns.

From the Norman Conquest until about 1500 the principles of internal environmental design changed little. Heating buildings was a major concern, and daylight and ventilation were enabled by narrow plan buildings. If buildings were larger than a house, such as an inn, college, or castle, they were built around courtyards to maintain the benefits of a narrow plan. The sixteenth century also saw the invention of the chimney, to provide an effective and convenient way of exhausting smoke at a higher level than a mere hole in the centre of the roof. Early chimneys were expensive status symbols, and were added to the fronts of houses to show off the owners' ability to afford them.

In some vernacular traditions, such as in the Lake District, elaborate chimneys took on a significance

William Grevel's house (c.1380), Chipping Camden, Gloucestershire.

Vicars' Close, Wells, Somerset: medieval stone terraced houses, fourteenth century with later chimneys.

Typical medieval windows.

that far outweighed their function, which was often compromised. Lake District yeomen built large, elaborate circular chimneys to impress and outdo their neighbours – but the internal flues were still square in section, and so inefficient that they had to wear their hats indoors to avoid being covered in soot. This was such a constant risk when warming oneself in front of the fire that it became known as the 'hallan drop', named after the 'hallan', or entrance hall, on the other side of the chimney.

THE NEXT 300 YEARS: TUDOR TO REGENCY

The medieval age passed, first into a transitional phase, and then into the beginnings of the modern age. Economic prosperity from increased trade and exploration of the world in Tudor times also wrought immense social and economic changes. The Reformation allowed more freedom of thought, and redistributed church wealth to a new capitalist class. The destruction of the medieval guilds removed labour restraints on trade and the modern era began. However, in terms of houses and energy there was little immediate change. Brick became a more common building material, resulting in a standard brick size being established by the Worshipful Company of Tylers and Bricklayers in 1571. Glass was also readily available, at the top end of the market at least; this enabled Elizabethan mansions to be built with large glazed windows, criss-crossed with brick glazing bars, or mullions and transoms, such as Hardwick Hall – 'Hardwick Hall more glass than wall'.

The late sixteenth century saw the first attempts at what could be called town planning, as various proclamations such as the London Act of 1580 attempted to stem the urban sprawl around London. The intention was not to create a green belt, but to stop the potential spread of plague between close-packed dwellings. Sadly this prescient Act did not prevent the Great Plague and the Great Fire of London in the latter half of the following century. Further legislation sought to

Townend farmhouse, Troutbeck, Windermere, 1628.

Hardwick Hall, Derbyshire, 1590.

control aspects of building, and influenced architectural development throughout the seventeenth century, starting with a Poor Law Act in 1601 making the payment of rates compulsory. The Hearth Tax came into effect in 1662, which levied a charge on the number of hearths in a home. Unsurprisingly, after the Great Fire of London in 1666, the following year saw a City of London Building Act to increase fire resistance and party-wall construction between dwellings.

A window tax was levied on all but the poorest homes in 1696; it was replaced by another version of the window tax in 1747. This latter tax goes some way to explain the phenomenon of 'blind windows' in façades, where a former window was blocked up to avoid the tax, or designed to complete the architectural symmetry of the composition while avoiding window tax. The window tax was later trebled in 1797 to pay for the war with France. Further London Building Acts were imposed in the early eighteenth century, concerned with the fire risk of materials used on

façades, and prescribing a 4in setback for windows in an attempt to avoid the spread of flames from one house to the next.

Brick taxes were introduced in 1784 and increased in 1794 and 1803, being repealed for tiles in 1833, and finally completely repealed in 1850. Various ingenious techniques were invented to avoid the brick tax, such as 'mathematical tiles' – no doubt taking advantage of the 1833 relaxation for tiles. Mathematical tiles are vertically hung tiles designed to look like brickwork – the kudos of brick construction without the tax! No doubt the brick tax was finally repealed because brick construction became so commonplace after the coming of the railways in the nineteenth century – and the use of local vernacular materials began to decline due to cheap transportation afforded by the canals and then the railways.

The London Building Act of 1774, and other similar local Acts that followed, heralded the era of building regulations as we might recognize them today.

This Act became known as the 'Black Act' because of the impositions and prescriptions that it contained. It was a consolidation of the Building Acts since the fire of 1666, and included the following prescriptions for houses:

- Houses should be brick with no wooden decoration.
- Windows should be recessed behind brick façades.
- Roofs should be slate and should not overhang, i.e. parapet walls.
- Four 'classes' of house were stipulated, e.g. first rate to fourth rate.
- The thickness of brick walls was prescribed, tapering to the top.

The Act led to standardization and the publication of 'pattern books' that presented various architectural ideas and compositions that complied with legislation. It was also largely instrumental in creating the legacy of fine Georgian urban architecture in this country. Rural houses were also influenced by Georgian ideas of architectural composition, and many vernacular houses were altered to reflect the geometry of urban houses and large country houses – usually with a central front door and symmetrical windows.

The dictates of standardization and fashion had their downside, as regional vernacular styles, often forged over centuries in response to local climate and conditions for good practical reasons, were largely lost. The parapet wall is a very good example, prescribed in the London Act to prevent the overhanging roofs of close-knit dwellings from aiding the spread of fire from one house to another. However, the parapet is not a good architectural response to the climate of the British Isles in general, and is particularly impractical in areas of wind-driven rain and high exposure, such as most of the west of the islands. Many problems of dampness in old houses are due to parapet walls, since it is far more logical to take the roof over the top of the wall to shelter it from our wet climate.

In Georgian times building elements became highly refined, particularly windows. The double-hung sash window remains an exceptionally good design for ventilation, as it can be opened from both the top and the bottom to give openings at ceiling level to allow hot air to escape, while the lower opening allows cooler air to come into the room. The principal rooms in the Georgian house also had high ceilings to allow for good ventilation and daylight penetration. The greater availability of glass and technology allowed for larger windows, and the typical Georgian house had around half of its main façade taken up by glazing – an optimal amount, particularly when orientated to the south to benefit from solar gains.

The chimney was now ubiquitous, after its invention in the 1500s and its development from a status symbol on houses to a common feature, to allow for the convenience of a fireplace in every room, particularly after the repeal of the Hearth Tax in 1689. While it was possible to have more than one fireplace in a room, or several in a large room, the proportions of rooms in houses were limited not only by traditional timber and masonry construction, but also by the area or volume that could reasonably be heated by a fireplace.

THE VICTORIAN AND EDWARDIAN PERIODS

The industrial revolution produced new materials and required new building types, made possible by new materials. Larger buildings could be built that were not a series of courtyards, but deeper plan buildings could not necessarily rely on daylight or natural ventilation. Advances in the use of building materials and structural engineering were accompanied by advances in other fields: in the realm of artificial lighting, the first gas lighting from coal and tar was installed in offices in Whitehaven in 1765, which was a port second only to London at that time. By 1789 gas was being made and stored at Birmingham, and Pall Mall in London was lit by gas street lamps in 1820. However, the House of Commons was still being illuminated by 240 candles in the 1840s, and although gas lighting was experimented with, it was not pursued due to its great expense. It was only in the 1850s that gas lighting was widely installed for lighting in buildings, and later still before it became common in houses. Even so, there were some Members of Parliament who still argued that candles were much better. Electricity was first used to light a house in 1880, but did not become widespread until after 1900.

The population of England quadrupled from 10 million at the beginning of the nineteenth century to

Bedford Square, London.

Georgian rural house.

40 million at its end. This historically unprecedented growth was made possible by the prosperity of advanced industrialization, but it had inherent social penalties wrought by rapid urbanization, such as overcrowding and squalor. On the eve of World War I, 80 per cent of England's population lived in cities, largely because agricultural decline, exacerbated by policies of free trade with consequent cheap imports of prairie wheat, caused a rural exodus to the cities. Furthermore, the spread of the railway network enabled cheap and swift migration from rural areas to new industrial employment opportunities in towns and cities, particularly after a Railway Bill was passed in 1823 allowing trains to carry passengers. Conversely, systematic suburbanization allowed the emergent middle classes to escape city centres, contrary to trends in continental Europe.

Technological progress in the glass and iron industries permitted larger roofs that could be glazed, initially for buildings such as the Palm House at Kew in 1844 and the Great Exhibition Hall of 1851, later dubbed the Crystal Palace. These innovations allowed deep-plan spaces that could be daylit, such as railway station concourses. Gradually, such technology filtered down to domestic uses, allowing larger panes of glass at an economic price. Ventilation was still an inhibiting factor in architectural development, and dictated very high ceiling heights to allow for adequate cross ventilation in buildings such as schools and large houses. The Victorians employed some ingenious ventilation methods in their large buildings before the advent of mechanical ventilation and air conditioning. The tower of Big Ben was initially conceived as a ventilation tower.

Political emancipation began with the First Reform Act of 1832 and was then compounded by subsequent Acts. Continental socialism was gradually imported, but at first in an idealistic guise when compared to the bloodshed in mainland Europe – in the form of practical Liberalism. Utopian socialism proved a strong cultural and artistic catalyst amongst the artists and architects of the Arts and Crafts Movement in the late nineteenth and early twentieth century. The rise of the middle classes, coupled with economically competitive education, spurred on the rise of the professions. Political reaction to the consolidated success of the Liberal Party found cogent form in two speeches by

Disraeli, who was the undisputed leader of the Conservatives by 1872. These tellingly concentrated on social health legislation, and the first compared the biblical quotation 'Vanitas vanitatum, omnia vanitas' with his contemporary adage 'Sanitas sanitatum, omnia sanitas' ('Vanity of vanities, all is vanity' (Ecclesiastes 1:2): thus 'Sanity of sanities, all is sanity' – or 'sanitation').

> Pure air, pure water, the inspection of unhealthy habitations, the adulteration of food – these and many kindred matters may be legitimately dealt with by the legislature ... the first consideration of a minister should be the health of the people.[1]

This Latin analogy heralded the political acceptance of the new 'religion' of sanitation, and the gradual recognition of the dire social consequences of *laissez-faire* capitalism. Although a Public Health Act was passed in 1848, allowing the creation of local by-laws, the legislation was relatively ineffective compared with later consolidating acts, such as Disraeli's 1875 Public Health Act. The political importance of sanitation was symbolically emphasized by 'The Great Stink' of 1858, during which the stench of the open sewer that the Thames had become, emptied the House of Commons – not to mention deaths from widespread diseases such as cholera, which peaked in mid-century. Dr John Snow's evidence for the waterborne transmission of disease was reinforced when Prince Albert died of typhus in 1861, attributed to 'bad drains' – a fact that undoubtedly helped to stimulate concentration on improved sanitary legislation.[2]

National wealth in the United Kingdom increased six-fold in the nineteenth century, however middle-class wealth was always comparatively modest, and rented accommodation, rather than owner occupation, was by far the norm. The sheer number of houses in England and Wales rose from one million in the late eighteenth century to several million by the eve of World War I. Although by no means all of these were designed by architects, most of them were little more than slums housing the new urban workforce. About nine out of ten people rented their homes from private landlords, including many of the middle and professional classes.

Architecture displayed a polarity similar to other

fields of Victorian endeavour, notably symbolized by the battle of the styles between the Gothic Revival and Classicism in public buildings. However, the absence of historical precedents in either of these two styles for economic middle-class housing opened the way for the revival of vernacular styles of domestic architecture. This stylistic approach to houses was exemplified by architects such as Richard Norman Shaw (1831–1912), who usually operated at the top end of the market, but also produced higher density semi-detached villas in burgeoning garden suburbs, such as Bedford Park, Chiswick, in the late 1870s.

The new battle for the domestic suburban market was a fierce one between speculative builders and the rapidly increasing ranks of professional architects – by the 1870s, architects were using the new religion of sanitation as a major weapon in their armoury. The RIBA advised the local government board on the drafting of model by-laws: these were the forerunners of modern building regulations and dealt with sanitation, amongst other matters such as structural and space standards, and were published in 1877. Such collaboration was thought to inspire public confidence in professionals, and resulted in a technical handbook rather than basic prescriptions – also presumably to the loss of the speculative builders in general.[3]

Such technical matters as ventilation and plumbing became equal to aesthetic preoccupations, leading another famous artist-architect, Philip Webb (1831–1915), to say 'Now this is so beautiful I don't like it to be covered up', upon inspection of a new domestic drainage system![4] The promotion of the 'artistic house' garnered the middle to higher end of the suburban market for architects, and builders sought to superficially emulate the aesthetics and styles of these vanguard dwellings in cheaper, mass-housing schemes. Ultimately the trinity of sanitation, planning and artistic aesthetics was adapted to lesser budgets and pervaded burgeoning middle-class suburbia.

By 1900, British domestic architecture reached an apogee recognized by the rest of Europe, and confirmed in Herman Muthesius' *The English House* in 1904. This domestic cultural peak was undoubtedly enabled by middle-class prosperity at the height of Empire, and virtually all of Muthesius' illustrated houses were far from modest. He reported that:

There is nothing as unique in English architecture as the development of the house … no nation is more committed to its development because no nation has identified itself more with the house.

About a third of Britain's dwellings were erected between 1800 and 1911 (several million houses), and a third of them between 1870 and 1911. Traditional domestic construction techniques did not change significantly over the period 1840–1919, apart from obvious improvements due to improved building regulations, sanitation and local by-laws. The large amount of Victorian housing that has survived has done so not just because it is flexible, but because it is popular with the general public. Strong local building and materials traditions continued until late in the nineteenth century, and it was only in the early twentieth century that brick-making became a national industry and regional production petered out. In architectural terms local materials gave us the variety of brick colours such as Luton 'purples', Reading 'silver-greys' and Staffordshire 'blues'.

The construction quality of Victorian housing was not immune from bad workmanship, but the stock that has survived for well over a hundred years must be the best. No age is free from construction mistakes, but at the end of the nineteenth century there were frequent comments about improved construction, even in small houses. Building regulations and local by-laws did not eradicate bad construction, but they seemed to reduce the scope for it. In terms of materials, Portland cement (patented in 1824) was universally used for all foundations and drainage-pipe joints by the late nineteenth century. Damp-proof courses were introduced from around 1850, and from 1890 all new housing in Manchester used them – by 1900 new buildings almost invariably included them. Floorboards were no longer permitted to lie on the ground, even in small houses, from the 1860s–1870s onwards, heralding ubiquitous perforated 'air bricks' to ventilate suspended floors.[5]

Housing standards generally improved over the nineteenth century, led by model housing prototypes such as those exhibited at the Great Exhibition in 1852 and funded by Prince Albert, and successful industrialists such as George Cadbury's model village at Bourneville near Birmingham. Such enlightened

Typical ribbon development.

industrialists realized that productivity could be increased by providing decent dwellings for their employees, alongside new factories sited on the edges of conurbations. These early schemes led to the 'garden city' concept championed by Ebenezer Howard and realized in Welwyn and Letchworth in the early twentieth century. Social, technological and legislative progress also generally improved the housing stock, with improved by-laws and mandatory measures such as damp-proof coursing and cavity walls.

TWENTIETH-CENTURY HOUSING

The end of World War I provided the catalyst for mass social housing in Britain. Lloyd George promised 'homes fit for heroes' for returning combatants, after the generally poor health of the working population recruited to fight the war was publicized. The Walter's report in 1918 recommended that local authorities should be subsidised to build housing for rent, at lower densities than the average in Victorian terraced housing. Over four million dwellings were built in council estates during the inter-war years. Due to the shortage of skilled labour and essential materials, about a quarter of a million dwellings of this new housing stock were constructed by non-traditional methods. Among the new methods of construction that were developed were more than twenty steel-framed housing systems, along with other systems based on pre-cast and in situ concrete, timber, and occasionally cast iron.

Inter-war private housing developments were usually of a lower density, causing problems of 'ribbon' and 'pepper-pot' development, made possible by low petrol prices. Ribbon developments were only one house deep and along arterial roads, and exacerbated the perception of housing incursion into rural areas, among other problems. Pepper-pot developments, on the other hand, made vehicular access more difficult, as they were isolated houses in rural locations. The sprawling, suburban housing boom of the 1920s and

1930s invaded the British landscape like the tentacles of an octopus, which inspired the title of an influential book by Clough Williams-Ellis. The architect of Portmeirion created the catalyst for new legislation with his book *England and the Octopus*, published in 1928. The provocatively argued book started a polemic that led to the passing of the Prevention of Ribbon Development Act and the London Green Belt Act shortly afterwards. They were the precursors of the modern planning system.[6]

The aftermath of World War II created an even greater need for mass housing development, not to mention the need to rebuild housing damaged by enemy aircraft. The Ministry of Health predicted the future housing demand in early 1943, and a strategy to cope with estimated post-war demand was devised at the beginning of 1944. The Reconstruction Committee's proposal involved a three-staged timetable, starting with an emergency period for the first few years to try and house all those who needed accommodation; the following five years would concentrate on new housing construction; and the final period of ten years was aimed at replacing sub-standard and slum housing.

In the initial emergency period of two years it was hoped that nearly half-a-million permanent dwellings would be provided — it was belatedly agreed that this would include around 200,000 dwellings with a short and finite design life. The Burt and Dudley committees were convened in 1942 to consider non-traditional construction techniques to overcome labour and skills shortages, and planning and space standards to reflect lifestyle changes, respectively. Social surveys revealed that the vast majority of the population preferred a small detached house or bungalow over a flat.

More prosaically, the only possible answer to the sheer scale and scope of post-war housing demand was seen as prefabrication. The problems were different from those faced after the first war, in that material shortages were less crucial than the supply of skilled labour. In addition, the surplus of steel and aluminium production caused by the war effort dictated housing experimentation with such materials. The most ubiquitous type of steel-framed house was the British Iron and Steel Federation (BISF) house designed by the architect Frederick Gibberd, while the Airey and Wate's houses were typical of the concrete

systems. The aircraft industry contributed lightweight, aluminium-framed and clad systems, such as the AIROH (Aircraft Industries' Research Organisation on Housing) bungalow and the ARCON house.[7] (ARCON stands for 'architectural consultants', and was a practice of architects who worked closely with companies such as ICI and Turners Asbestos Cement Co Ltd.)

The decades following World War II saw the philosophy of house construction changing towards that of industrialized building, with as much work as possible transferred from the site to the factory. However, public confidence waned after the Ronan Point collapse in 1968, which involved large panel, off-site construction. High-rise housing buildings were already controversial for social reasons, but Ronan Point raised technical doubts as well. Ronan Point was a twenty-two-storey point-block with an inherently strong structure, but it was not designed to withstand the large gas explosion that caused its partial collapse. The explosion occurred in a corner flat on the eighteenth floor and caused the floors above to lift, and the panels were blown outwards leading to progressive collapse. Other construction problems were found in some of the other large panel buildings.

Volumetric systems using a series of prefabricated 'boxes' that were connected on site, were also used during the sixties and seventies. For ease of transportation, these usually involved lightweight timber or metal frames – following on from earlier volumetric aluminium bungalows from the immediate post-war period.

CONCLUSIONS

Climate change, due to the carbon dioxide emissions from human activities, is recognized as scientific fact. Extreme weather events, such as storms and floods, are increasing in frequency, and such trends were recognized by the insurance industry several years ago. Roughly half of the energy and carbon dioxide emissions in the UK are accounted for by buildings, and roughly half of this is from our houses. The UK government is attempting to reduce the country's carbon dioxide emissions by 20 per cent of 1990 levels by 2010, and by 60 per cent by 2050. Energy from renewable sources forms a significant portion of this strategy, and the retention of old buildings is recognized as the most energy-efficient form of property development. They contain significant 'embodied energy' in their already manufactured fabric, historic craftsmanship and labour, and local materials. The transport costs alone, possibly from the other side of the world, of replacing historic fabric are significant, particularly when compared to the historic costs of the local materials used in older buildings.

Recent estimates suggest that in order to reduce carbon dioxide emissions by 60 per cent by 2050, in line with international governmental agreements such as the Kyoto Protocol, nearly half-a-million existing dwellings would have to be refurbished each year in the UK. Over a third of the UK housing stock was built before 1940, and two-thirds before 1965. The most common house is the semi-detached (5 million – 30 per cent of stock), followed by purpose-built low-rise flats and detached houses.

The rate of owner-occupation has increased from 10 per cent in 1914 to 70 per cent in 2007. Roughly half of the UK construction industry expenditure relates to the repair, refurbishment and maintenance of the existing building stock. New building stock only adds about 1 per cent to the stock each year. Existing housing is where the necessary energy and environmental improvements will be made to combat climate change, global warming, and potentially increasing energy bills.

The continued occupation of existing houses, combined with energy performance improvement measures, is both inevitable and desirable. In fact, the best and most economical time to improve energy efficiency is in the context of refurbishment, extension, restoration or conservation of existing houses. To demolish them is a waste of embodied energy and finite resources. Case studies suggest that simple packages of measures can cost effectively improve the energy and environmental performance of typical Victorian terraces and later semi-detached houses to modern standards.

The past century has seen the most unprecedented advances in material lifestyles for most people, especially in the developed world, and not least in our domestic lives and houses. Although we think of the Victorians as great engineers and architects in an advanced society, they largely lived in an age without electricity. Although electricity was a technology that existed at the end of the Victorian age, and the Houses of Parliament eventually had electric lighting installed in 1881, we are now using well over ten times as much energy from fossil fuels as the average Edwardian in our houses alone. In 1890 there were only about two dozen houses that even had electric lighting, and they were the grandest of houses such as Cragside in Northumberland, designed by Richard Norman Shaw for the industrialist Sir William Armstrong.

Taking a wider perspective, humankind has only had the convenience of electricity for the past 100 years out of the last 10,000, and only the last 2,000 years are viewed as civilization. As the Victorian age ended, the growth of modern energy use in our buildings and houses really began. The lighting, mechanically ventilating and air conditioning industries took off, using fans and pumps powered by electricity to light, heat and cool our buildings. Today we regard electricity as indispensable, but we can use less of it and other fossil fuels by exploiting some simple means to make ourselves more environmentally sustainable in our homes. Those who live in old houses can at least take some comfort from the fact that they are already living within a potentially sustainable domestic environment. The life cycle of a modern building is viewed as about sixty years, with luck, so the typical Victorian terraced house which is now over 100 years old has already proved its sustainability. However, its energy performance may need improvement to ensure that it continues to be environmentally sustainable for another 100 years, and it is possible to do this economically.

Old houses are a non-renewable resource that should be treated as such. Many old houses, and not just those that are listed and in conservation areas, give a special character to our built environment. They are architecturally and historically important, and their materials and methods of construction are no longer in common use. This makes them perform in a different way to modern buildings and materials, and they require sympathetic additions and adaptations. Generally, houses built with solid walls need to 'breathe', as they will absorb moisture from rainfall but also release it through evaporation if the original designs of ventilation paths and construction techniques are retained.

Most modern houses operate on quite different principles, as the introduction of the cavity wall in about 1920 started the change in construction technology to try to totally exclude moisture from dwellings and other building types. The cavity wall was originally intended as a rainscreen to improve levels of comfort afforded by the hopefully continuously dry inner leaf of construction. The air space in an empty cavity wall also provides some thermal insulation, and gradually the process of filling some of the cavity with insulation began. But fully filling a cavity wall in a refurbishment can have technical risks if the wrong materials are used in inappropriate contexts. If the cavity is fully bridged, moisture may travel through to the interior.

Equally, the inappropriate application of modern construction techniques to old houses can reduce or completely remove the ability of their fabric to 'breathe'. For example, the application of an impervious material such as Portland cement render to the wall of an old house that was built to 'breathe' can trap moisture in the old walls and cause endless problems of dampness and spalling render, stone, or brickwork. Some basic understanding of the different building physics involved in a solid as opposed to a cavity wall construction is required before successful energy improvements can be made. As Peter Burberry puts it:

> It is depressing, at a time when highly sophisticated plant is being used for environmental control, to realize that throughout much of history, buildings themselves were highly developed examples of applied science, achieving high levels of performance even when designers could not define or quantify the factors that they took into account.[8]

The important and sensitive nature of many older buildings and their fabric demands that work on them:
- is carried out in an appropriate and compatible manner;
- takes proper account of the way they were constructed and were intended to perform;
- causes the minimum amount of intervention;
- and is reversible whenever possible.

There are simple ways of improving the energy efficiency of all old houses, which include the following:

- improving building fabric, such as increased thermal insulation;
- improving windows, such as double-glazing, or secondary glazing;
- using efficient boilers and heating systems;
- installing better controls, e.g. for heating and lighting;
- using long-life, energy-efficient light bulbs;
- limiting excessive air infiltration by draught-stripping – bearing in mind the need for controlled ventilation in many old construction types;
- ensuring better management of existing systems;
- undertaking effective preventive maintenance and repairs.

Most of these can be applied without adversely affecting fabric and contents, even in buildings which cannot be physically altered owing to their significance, their condition, or their sensitivity. It is very seldom that there is absolutely nothing you can do to improve the energy efficiency of an old house cost effectively.

SUMMARY

- Archaeological evidence shows that most of the Roman villas scattered around the countryside had underfloor heating, or hypocausts.
- Medieval timber-framed buildings were reasonably comfortable, and with enough straw the thatched roof might even match the thermal properties of a modern roof. Even the infill of the timber framing, made of wattle, mud, straw and animal hair, might be built up enough to provide modest levels of thermal insulation.
- The development of the English house is indebted to the Normans and the stone buildings they created, first in the form of castles for defence. Massive stone constructions such as cathedrals and castles are wonderfully cool and comfortable in summer. The thick stone walls are able to absorb heat energy and store it to give it out again later during the cooler night. This thermal mass is less useful in winter, however, as it means that heating energy is also being absorbed by stone walls rather than heating the occupants.

- Glass did not become readily available for buildings that were not special ones until the seventeenth and eighteenth centuries. Before that time even important buildings might have animal skins or waxed paper as makeshift glazing in their windows.
- From the Norman Conquest until about 1500 the principles of internal environmental design changed little. Heating buildings was a major concern. Daylighting and ventilation were provided by narrow plan buildings.
- The sixteenth century also saw the invention of the chimney. Early chimneys were expensive status symbols, and added to the fronts of houses to show off the owners' ability to afford them.
- The Hearth Tax came into effect in 1662, which levied a charge on the number of hearths in a home. A City of London Building Act was passed in 1667 to increase fire resistance and party-wall construction between dwellings.
- The London Building Act of 1774, and other similar local acts that followed, heralded the era of building regulations as we might recognize them today. This act became known as the 'Black Act' because of the impositions and prescriptions that it contained, but it is largely responsible for the legacy of Georgian urban, domestic architecture that we have today.
- Many problems of dampness in old houses are due to parapet walls. It is far more logical to take the roof over the top of the wall to shelter it from our wet climate.
- The rise of surburbia, and that most ubiquitous of British domestic forms, the semi-detached house, began with the increase in urban populations in the nineteenth century.

- About a third of Britain's dwellings were erected between 1800 and 1911 (several million houses), and a third of them between 1870 and 1911. Traditional domestic construction techniques did not change significantly over the period 1840–1919.
- The end of World War I provided the catalyst for mass social housing in Britain. Lloyd George promised 'homes fit for heroes' for returning combatants.
- Generally, houses built with solid walls need to 'breathe', as they will absorb moisture from rainfall, but will also release it through evaporation if the originally designed ventilation paths and construction techniques are retained. Most modern houses operate on quite different principles, as the introduction of the cavity wall in about 1920 started the change in construction technology to try to totally exclude moisture from dwellings and other building types.
- There are simple ways of improving the energy efficiency of all old houses, such as improving building fabric; increasing thermal insulation; improving windows, by installing double glazing or secondary glazing; using efficient boilers and heating systems; installing better controls, e.g. for heating and lighting; using long-life, energy-efficient light bulbs; limiting excessive air infiltration by draught-stripping – bearing in mind the need for ventilation in many old construction types; ensuring better management of existing systems; undertaking effective preventive maintenance and repairs.

CHAPTER 2

Medieval, Tudor and Stuart: Before 1700

OVERVIEW

Many houses built before 1700 in Great Britain are listed buildings, as they are invariably comparatively rare survivals. They have certainly already proved their sustainability credentials by surviving for some centuries – not to mention the embodied energy contained in medieval houses, invariably derived from local materials and local labour. Wood is a renewable resource, and most houses built before 1500 were small timber-framed houses. The country was still covered in large tracts of woodland, and most houses were rudimentary shelters, the simplest being a cruck-frame. Only the best of these timber-framed houses have survived, and they are usually the more elaborate and grander examples.

Opportunities for improving energy and environmental performance are largely restricted to increasing loft insulation, carefully improving air leakage, and installing improved technology, such as lighting, heating and controls. Many medieval houses, particularly

Alms houses (1612), Chipping Camden, Gloucestershire.

more modest survivals with limited protection, will have sustained damage due to inappropriate or inadequate repairs and maintenance at some stage in their history. Inept attempts to improve medieval buildings, in terms of their energy efficiency or otherwise, show the importance of proper research and professional advice when undertaking work to ancient houses.

An understanding of how traditional building materials work is essential. Those medieval houses that have survived, have usually done so because they are the best of their type in terms of quality of construction. And they were usually carefully conserved over the centuries, or 'saved' in more recent times. William Morris, the great Victorian whose wallpaper and fabric designs still enjoy commercial success, when forming the Society for the Protection of Ancient Buildings (SPAB) in 1877, drew upon the conservation philosophy of another great Victorian, John Ruskin:

> … that it is again no question of expediency or feeling whether we shall preserve the buildings of past times or not. *We have no right whatever to touch them.* They are not ours. They belong partly to those who built them, and partly to all the generations of mankind who are to follow us. The dead have still there right in them … we have no right to obliterate …[1]

Or to put it in biblical terms, when dealing with old houses:

Sicut serpentes, Sicut columbae
Be ye wise as serpents, and harmless as doves
Matthew 10 v.16

HEATING AND VENTILATION

Most medieval houses are constructed of timber frames, usually oak or elm, and their survival is invariably due to adequate and possibly excessive ventilation. Moisture and dampness are the enemies of all buildings, but particularly those made of wood. But all traditional building materials such as stone, brick, limewash and lime-based mortars and plaster absorb

Typical medieval timber-framed house, Hertfordshire.

more moisture than modern building materials – so they need sufficient ventilation to get rid of this moisture during dry spells. It is really only in modern times that we have sought to make our houses totally impervious to the elements. Historic houses need to 'breathe' in order to dry out their fabric by allowing absorbed moisture to evaporate.

When modern impervious materials are incorrectly applied to ancient houses, there is a risk of structural damage due to excessive moisture – and invariably there is a risk of unsightly damage to materials such as stone and soft brickwork that is incorrectly repointed using impervious Portland cement rather than lime mortar. Applying a render coat of cement rather than limewash to an old house is akin to wearing a plastic coat rather than a breathable Goretex jacket on a long walk – you should be comfortable in the latter, but

36

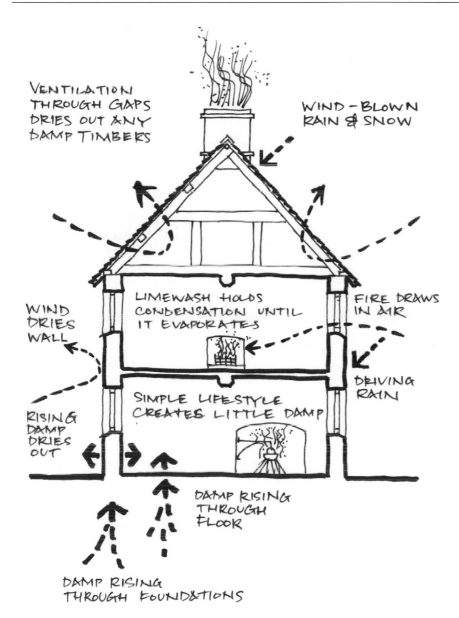

Cross-section through an old house, showing how moisture moves through the air and structure.

VENTILATION THROUGH GAPS DRIES OUT ANY DAMP TIMBERS

WIND-BLOWN RAIN & SNOW

LIMEWASH HOLDS CONDENSATION UNTIL IT EVAPORATES

FIRE DRAWS IN AIR

WIND DRIES WALL

DRIVING RAIN

RISING DAMP DRIES OUT

SIMPLE LIFESTYLE CREATES LITTLE DAMP

DAMP RISING THROUGH FLOOR

DAMP RISING THROUGH FOUNDATIONS

will get very sweaty in the former. The need for adequate and controlled ventilation is increased when ancient houses are subjected to an increase in humidity caused by our modern lifestyles, such as the increased water vapour from:

- occupants spending more time inside their houses nowadays;
- bathing, particularly showers;
- cooking;
- water tanks within the roof that are not fitted with lids.

At the same time, we reduce natural ventilation in old houses by:

- installing double or secondary glazing;
- no longer using open fires;
- blocking up disused fireplaces and flues.

Tudor chimney, Hatfield Old Palace, Hertfordshire, c1485.

We generally demand much higher comfort conditions in our houses these days, and certainly more than occupants would have enjoyed decades, let alone centuries ago. For example, there is no history of heating, let alone central heating, in buildings before 1790. Many early medieval houses would have had an open fire in the centre with a hole in the roof to, hopefully, allow the smoke to escape. The invention of chimneys, much celebrated in architectural terms in Tudor times, would have reduced smoky interiors to an extent. However, fireplaces were a luxury that took the chill off spaces, rather than fully warming them, and they also needed a great deal of ventilation to provide air for combustion of the fire.

Generally, our ancestors in medieval times dressed warmly with heavy clothes, even when inside, and sat in heavily upholstered furniture close to the radiant heat from a fireplace – if they were lucky. We have grown used to occupying our houses in our shirt sleeves and relying on luxurious levels of heating. A change of lifestyle, to some extent, may be necessary to inhabit some medieval houses – possibly analogous to the thrill of driving a convertible sports car! Good fun if you are well wrapped up, and have provided for inclement weather.

Medieval houses will usually be draughty to have survived relatively intact from the potential ravages of rot caused by dampness, but there is a difference between ventilation and what is known as air infiltration: the former is considered controllable, while the latter causes air leaks and draughts. Timber-framed medieval houses are probably more susceptible to infiltration than stone ones, as there is more scope for cracks between framing and infills such as wattle and daub, which shrinks when it dries out – apart from vernacular building traditions, such as in the Lake District, where drystone walls were used for dwellings – although these walls are invariably now rendered. However, there is often a danger of treating the symptoms rather than the causes when dealing with old houses.

Case Study 2.1 (*see* page 42) clearly shows that a simplistic approach, such as the assumption that air leaks and draughts are around windows and doors, is often misguided, and that adequate research, such as an air-pressure test of a medieval dwelling, can help to gain an understanding of how the building is performing. And allow for the design of an optimal amount of natural ventilation, rather than random and excessive air infiltration that leads to occupants' discomfort.

Conversely, some research leads to romantic notions of how our forbears lived. British Gas recently surveyed sixteenth-century dwellings and discovered that they leaked about 10cu m of air an hour for every square metre of wall area, on average – as compared to modern dwellings, which leaked from 15–40cu m. Apparently the reason for this was that the medieval timber-framed houses were made more airtight with stones and wattle and daub, used to fill up cracks. And one can certainly imagine the process of continuous improvement to the buildings' fabric, undertaken by successive generations of inhabitant in search of comfort. However, the assertion that Tudor homes 'leak less energy' may be premature:

Wind turbines, solar panels and other high tech green devices may get the media attention. But the smartest way to save energy may be to live in a Tudor house and insulate the attic and repair the windows.

Hank Dittmar, Chief Executive of the Prince's
Foundation for the Built Environment, 1999

Despite this optimistic view of medieval houses, there is invariably a range of sympathetic and sensitive energy efficiency improvements to make when living in a medieval house.

Good Management

Good management measures would include maintaining equipment properly; setting controls correctly; switching equipment off when it is not in use; adopting appropriate modern technologies; and carefully considered draughtproofing to avoid excessive air infiltration.

Controls Improvements

In particular it is important to improve temperature and time controls, and to add heating zone controls to avoid overheating unoccupied rooms. One of the most effective ways to save energy is to turn the heating down – for which it helps to have a means of control to start with! Typically, a room thermostat might be set to around 21°C (70°F), but if this is reduced to

Typical room thermostat.

20°C (68°F), heating energy consumption can be reduced by 6–10 per cent. Wearing warmer clothing and reducing the temperature to 19°C (66°F) or even 18°C (64°F) will have corresponding savings. However, most medieval building fabric and fittings will need minimal temperature levels to conserve them. The National Trust does not allow the temperature of its properties to fall below 5°C (41°F) when they are empty and closed up for the winter, and pursues a strategy of 'conservation heating': this is a way of avoiding extremes of internal humidity by the control of temperature.[2]

Conservation Heating

The National Trust has used the idea of 'conservation heating' since the 1980s to ensure a balance between temperature and humidity in its properties – this seldom raises the temperature by more than 5°C (10°F) above the outside temperature, which generally maintains a relative humidity (RH) of about 50–65 per cent – a good compromise for most materials. This is why radiators may sometimes be on in the summer if the weather is humid. Conversely, on a chilly, dry day in winter, after the NT's houses have been closed for the season, some visitors would find them far too cold for comfort. The amount of energy required is typically around a third of that required for 'comfort heating'. However, most NT properties are closed up for the winter with minimal heating levels, although some compromise between conservation and comfort heating may suit the occupants of ancient houses.

Insulation Improvements

Increases in insulation levels should be carefully considered, particularly in the roof. Insulation improvements to the floor and walls are usually more difficult, and may reduce the ability of the house to 'breathe'. Natural insulation materials, such as sheep's wool, are particularly sympathetic to medieval houses: wool is hygroscopic, which means that it allows moisture to pass through it, helping the house to 'breathe'. Like most traditional building materials, sheep's wool absorbs moisture during wet periods and then evaporates it in dry spells, thereby working in harmony with the ancient building fabric. But the introduction of impervious modern insulation may be detrimental, unless very carefully considered and detailed.

Typical medieval window with splayed reveals: Merton College, Oxford, 1375.

Windows and Doors Improvements

Usually the best course is to carefully consider draught-stripping to reduce infiltration, though this should not totally exclude natural ventilation. Obviously, original components should be retained and conserved. Replacement double glazing is usually completely inappropriate and will invariably destroy the original character of windows and doors. Secondary glazing is usually a good option, and SPAB advises that this should be removable and unobtrusive, and to use non-reflective glass.

Heating System Improvements

It is important to improve the efficiency of heating systems and thereby reduce fuel cost and consumption. Improvements to insulation levels, and optimizing natural ventilation levels, should result in a reduced heating boiler size. Technologies such as condensing boilers are worth considering. (A number of myths surround condensing boilers, but these are largely allayed in guidance from the Energy Saving Trust (EST). Their publication is downloadable from their website: CE 52 (GIL 74) *Domestic condensing boilers – the benefits and the myths.*)

Lighting Improvements

Low energy light bulbs are an easy and non-intrusive energy efficiency improvement to install in medieval houses.

WINDOWS

Windows invariably give character to a building, and especially so in medieval houses. Depending on the vernacular tradition, most medieval windows are smaller, with smaller panes of glass, than their modern equivalent. However, they usually had splayed reveals to disperse daylight to the interior, and were usually well displaced, providing adequate daylight even for a medieval library.

The installation of modern double glazing is unthinkable, and usually illegal in most medieval houses. Even if it were aesthetically desirable, it is rarely economical unless the existing timber window frames are in such a poor state of repair that replacement is essential. Plastic windows were often misguidedly placed in historic buildings, until more enlightened recent decades – this should certainly never be considered as an option in ancient houses, nor really in any old houses. uPVC windows are nearly always contradictory to the aesthetics of old houses due to the chunkiness of their glazing bars, and may need replacing after only twenty years. English Heritage maintains that it is cheaper to maintain and repair historic timber windows, than to replace them with plastic ones.

The survival of so many old timber window frames shows that they are long-lived when properly maintained and repaired. The importance of maintaining the appearance of appropriate glazing is recognized in Part L of the Building Regulations:

> The need to conserve the special characteristics of historic buildings needs to be recognised. The aim should be to improve energy efficiency where and to the extent that it is practicably possible, always provided that the work does not prejudice the character of the historic building, or increase the risk of long term deterioration to the building fabric or fittings. In arriving at an appropriate balance between historic building conservation and energy conservation, it would be appropriate to take into account the advice of the local planning authority's conservation officer.

Secondary glazing is usually the best option for medieval properties, as a second pane of glass or plastic, either fixed, removable or openable, installed on the inside of the existing window, leaves the original window relatively untouched. The optimum air gap for thermal insulation between the existing window and the secondary glazing is 20mm (¾in). The respective heritage organizations – English Heritage, Historic Scotland and Cadw in Wales – publish further

technical information about windows and other matters on their websites.

ROOFS

Thatched roofs are one of the most poignant and timeless sights of the British countryside, as thatch is the quintessentially medieval roofing material. There are about 50,000 houses with thatched roofs in this country, given that most old houses had their roof coverings altered when roofing slates and other industrialized materials became common with cheaper transport, along the canals and then the railways.

Roof ventilation is a crucial part of the ability for old houses to 'breathe', as the most moisture-laden air will be warm and will rise eventually into the roof space. Traditionally detailed slate or tile roofs will have ventilation gaps at the apex and either side of the base, or ridge and eaves – these will carry moisture away from the roof space and keep the structural roof timbers dry. However, the ventilation of many roof spaces is compromised by inappropriate impervious roofing felts and badly placed insulation retrofits – eventually these could lead to structural problems as damp timbers become rotten.

Insulation to medieval roof spaces requires careful thought, and possibly professional advice. Insulation placed at ceiling level makes the air in the roof space colder and can lead to condensation if the roof is not adequately ventilated. Insulation placed between rafters next to an impervious roof felt can also cause condensation, which will dampen the insulation – and care should be taken not to block up any ventilation gaps at the eaves and ridge of the roof. As many modern insulation materials retain moisture and do not dry out easily, natural materials such as sheep's wool are probably optimal for medieval roof spaces. It is also worth considering installing mechanical ventilation to kitchens and bathrooms to evacuate excessive moisture at its source.

Bats in the Belfry

Bats are a protected species, and the Wildlife and Countryside Act 1981 (WCA) protects bats and their roosts in England, Scotland and Wales. So if there is any chance of bats using your medieval roof space it is

Timber-framed thatched cottage.

best to do some research. Bats generally return to the same roosts every year, so these are protected whether bats are present or not. It is illegal to kill, injure or take a wild bat, or intentionally or recklessly damage, destroy or obstruct access to a bat roost. Having bats in the roof does not necessarily mean that building work, energy efficiency improvements, repairs or timber treatment are prohibited, but free advice should be obtained from the local Statutory Nature Conservation Organisation before proceeding. The Bat Conservation Trust has plenty of helpful information on its website: *www.bats.org.uk.*

CASE STUDIES

Case Study 2.1
Berg Cottage, Hertfordshire: listed seventeenth-century, timber-framed cottage.

Key points
- A National Trust cottage.
- Sensitive refurbishment to remove the causes of draughts, dampness and decay.
- Improvements in air tightness, which still allow the traditional construction to 'breathe'.
- Pressure tests revealed that the building fabric was still leaky, despite draught-stripping to walls and doors.
- Use of appropriate traditional methods and materials.
- Gas-fired condensing boiler heating system and room thermostats.
- Improvements in comfort levels for occupants.
- Fuel consumption and costs reduced by half.
- SAP rating improved from forty-nine to eighty-one.
- Carbon dioxide emissions reduced from 11.1 to 5.3 tonnes per year.

General

Berg Cottage was originally constructed in 1687; it is a Grade II listed building and is now owned by the National Trust. The cottage has a thatched roof, rendered timber-framed walls to the front elevation, and weatherboarding to the rear. It was still uncomfortable due to draughts, despite a retrofitted gas condensing boiler and radiator heating system. A chequered history of refurbishment included the inappropriate addition of impervious cement renders and paints in

LEFT: *Case Study 2.1 Berg cottage: front elevation.*

BELOW: *Case Study 2.1 Berg cottage: rear elevation.*

43

Case Study 2.1 Berg cottage: air pressure testing.

the 1930s: the use of Portland cement render rather than lime render did not allow the traditional fabric to 'breathe' and caused internal condensation and dampness, which led to structural damage to the timber frame. Air-pressure tests revealed a very draughty twenty-four air changes per hour, which is much more than necessary to prevent excessive moisture (the average in UK housing is around thirteen air changes per hour).

Windows

As the building was draughty there was a temptation to replace the windows, but the pressure test showed that the air leaks were mainly in the walls and roof of the house, rather than around the window openings. This test ensured that the budget was spent on effective improvements, instead of on unnecessary modifications.

Walls

The inappropriate Portland cement rendering was removed and replaced with lime render to the front elevation, taking the opportunity to install sheep's wool insulation to gaps between the timber frame. The weatherboarding to the rear was replaced after sheep's wool insulation and a vapour-permeable membrane were installed.

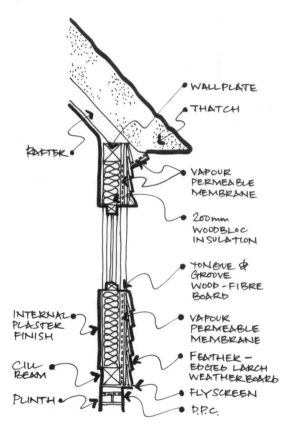

Case Study 2.1 Berg cottage: cross section through external wall.

Roof

The thatched roof was repaired to close the many small holes that were allowing air to leak in, causing draughts. During the pressure test a smoke pencil was used to find the source of draughts. Humidity-controlled fans were installed in the roof space, which would increase ventilation rates in the loft if humidity were high.

Berg cottage: rear elevation showing the installation of the vapour permeable membrane.

Case Study 2.2

Dolbelydr, Denbigh, North Wales: listed sixteenth-century gentry house.

Key points
- A Landmark Trust property.
- Architecturally important as it retains most of its original features.
- Historically important as the place where the first Welsh grammar was written.
- Thick limestone walls give a large amount of thermal mass, which makes the house comfortable in summer.
- Conservation from dereliction was a priority, and traditional materials and techniques were used.
- The roof was insulated using natural sheep's wool.
- Underfloor heating was added to the ground floor.
- Fuel consumption is not excessive compared to other Landmark Trust properties.

General

Dolbelydr is listed Grade II* for its historic interest as the home of the Elizabethan grammarian and physician, Henry Salesbury, who wrote the first Welsh grammar in 1593. Architecturally it is a good example of an intact end-chimney gentry house dating from around 1580. The house was still inhabited until the early twentieth century, after which it became derelict until conserved by the Landmark Trust recently. The external walls are 700mm (28in) thick limestone rubble, and the roof is constructed of sandstone tiles on an oak structure. The original floor is slate flags laid directly on to the ground. It was considered essential that all the natural materials were

Case Study 2.2 Dolbelydr: front elevation.

allowed to perform in their traditional way, allowing movement of moisture through the floor and walls – so adequate ventilation was also essential.

The house is sympathetically reused for holiday rental, which should generate enough income to ensure its future maintenance and survival.

Windows

The original window openings are few and small, and are divided with timber mullions and transoms; they contain single-glazed leaded windows (or 'lights'). The small windows are reminiscent of an age when winter comfort relied on reducing opportunities for draughts – an approach that still works in the house! In summer, through-ventilation is more than adequate for comfort, particularly when combined with the high thermal mass of the thick walls and stone roof – the 'cathedral cooling effect'. The walls are flush-pointed with lime mortar and protected with a shell-coat of limewash.

Walls

The walls are 700mm (28in) thick carboniferous limestone rubble. Any attempt to introduce a damp-proof course (dpc), either chemical or physical, would be foolhardy and entirely inappropriate in fact, such action would almost certainly be detrimental to both the building fabric and comfort conditions, because it would compromise the ability of the house to 'breathe'. Conservation was led by the use of traditional materials performing in a traditional way.

Roof

The original oak floor and roof timbers were retained where possible, but due to a century of neglect, some replacements were necessary. Most of the fallen oak roof trusses were craned back into place. Roof insulation takes the form of 50mm (2in) of natural sheep's wool – unfortunately, constraints such as headroom prevented the use of thicker amounts.

Case Study 2.2 Dolbelydr: interior.

Heating

The Landmark Trust has found that occupants unfortunately tend to turn any available heating thermostat controls up to a maximum: therefore holiday occupants can now only turn the heating on or off, while the thermostat control remains in the locked boiler house. This also prevents any unwitting damage to the fragile ancient fabric and fittings, such as desiccation from excessively low levels of humidity. Heating is water-borne from an oil-fired boiler to the underfloor heating system in the ground floor, set in lime mortar under the slate flags. The slate slabs are 50mm (2in) thick, set on lime mortar above a 100mm (4in) thick lime concrete slab, on 150mm (6in) of foamed clay pellets laid on bare earth. Panel radiators were placed in the first and attic storeys.

SUMMARY

- Many houses built before 1700 in Great Britain are listed buildings, as they are invariably comparatively rare survivals.
- Opportunities for improving energy and environmental performance are largely restricted to increasing loft insulation, carefully improving the control of air leakage, and the use of improved technology, such as lighting, heating and controls.
- An understanding of how traditional building materials work is essential.
- Most medieval houses are constructed of timber frames, usually oak or elm, and their survival is invariably due to adequate and possibly excessive ventilation.
- All traditional building materials, such as stone, brick, limewash and lime-based mortars and plaster, absorb more moisture than modern building materials – so they need sufficient ventilation to get rid of this moisture during dry spells.
- When modern impervious materials are incorrectly applied to ancient houses there is a risk of structural damage due to the retention of excessive moisture.
- We generally demand much higher comfort conditions in our houses these days, but some compromise is desirable when living in an ancient house.

- The difference between ventilation and air infiltration is important: the former is considered controllable, while the latter causes air leaks and draughts.
- Adequate research, such as an air-pressure test of a medieval dwelling, can help you gain an understanding of how the building is performing, and where the draughts and leaks are actually coming from.
- Energy efficiency improvements to medieval houses include the following: good management; controls; conservation heating; insulation; windows and doors; heating systems; and lighting.
- Windows invariably give character to a building, and especially so in medieval houses. The installation of modern double glazing is unthinkable, and usually illegal. Secondary glazing is an option, where an air gap of 20mm (¾in) is optimal for thermal insulation.
- Roof ventilation is a crucial part of the ability for old houses to 'breathe', as the most moisture-laden air will be warm and will rise eventually into the roof space.
- Insulation to medieval roof spaces requires careful thought, and possibly professional advice. Natural materials such as sheep's wool are probably optimal for medieval roof spaces.
- Bats are a protected species, and the Wildlife and Countryside Act 1981 (WCA) protects bats and their roosts in England, Scotland and Wales.
- The use of Portland cement render, rather than lime render, does not allow traditional fabric to 'breathe' and causes internal condensation and dampness, which can lead to structural damage.
- Underfloor heating, ideally combined with condensing boilers, is a good option for stone-constructed medieval houses due to the large amount of thermal mass in floor finishes such as stone paving slabs.
- The high internal temperatures generally demanded for modern comfort can damage medieval fabric and fittings, as relative humidity will drop below the ideal range of 50–65 per cent. Conversely, high levels of humidity will cause decay, so adequate ventilation is required to allow medieval houses to 'breathe'.

CHAPTER 3

Georgian: 1700–1837

OVERVIEW

The Georgian period of architecture officially began in 1714 with the ascent of George I to the throne, although the short reigns of Queen Anne (1700–14) and George IV (1825–37) are often included.

Grandiose front doors with fanlights above them are typical of Georgian houses, such as Hadley House in North London. The long Georgian period was not all mad kings, wigs and Hogarth's satirical depictions of gin palaces and debauchery: Georgian architecture is

Hadley House, Monken Hadley, North London, 1707.

Georgian doorway in old Hatfield, Hertfordshire.

inspired by Roman and Greek classical architecture in appearance and proportions. The Italian Renaissance of the sixteenth century had reinterpreted the architectural rules laid down by the ancients, and this neo-classicism was initially imported by British architects such as Inigo Jones (1573–1652) and Sir Christopher Wren (1632–1723). The latter architect's enthusiasm for classicism explains the adoption of a domed church for St Paul's Cathedral, although early designs were more Gothic than Classical in style. British domestic architecture was heavily inspired by the villas of the Italian stonemason and architect, Andrea Palladio (1508–80) – such as his Villa Rotondo at Vicenza, near Venice.

Palladianism dominated the start of this period, which ranged through to the Regency architectural

Villa Rotondo at Vicenza near Venice, by Andrea Palladio, 1569.

Georgian streetscape in old Hatfield, Hertfordshire.

Regency terraced houses in Cheltenham.

Regency terraced houses in Cheltenham.

Park Crescent in London, by John Nash, 1818.

style towards its end. The extremes of the latter style are epitomized by the Royal Pavilion in Brighton, with its references to the architecture of all points Eastern. Good examples of more modest, domestic, Regency architecture predominate in towns such as Cheltenham in Gloucestershire. Many of the crescents, squares and terraced streets in British towns and cities date from the Georgian era – such as those around Regent's Park in London by the architect John Nash (1752–1835). The population in Britain was expanding and becoming increasingly urban due to the start of the industrial revolution. Most Georgian houses are now sought-after properties, often in conservation areas, and many are listed buildings.

Most Georgian houses, in towns and cities at least, were speculatively built by developers employing sur-veyors, master builders and craftsmen. Architects were rarely employed on the modest, usually three-storey terraces that make up most Georgian townscapes, their talents being saved for more grandiose houses or unified terraced compositions. The uniformity of much Georgian architecture risks blandness, were it not for the neo-classical symmetry and harmonious proportions employed. Rural houses, which until then retained vernacular traditions, also began to get the Georgian treatment – which invariably meant a central entrance door and symmetrical windows. While it is unlikely that speculative Georgian build-ing developers envisaged their houses lasting for two or three centuries, usually only the best has survived and been conserved. That most ubiquitous of British house types, the semi-detached house, was also invented in the Georgian era, although it remained

53

Typical Georgian terraced housing in Dundalk, County Louth, Ireland.

the exception rather than the rule for another century or so.

The Great Fire of London in 1666 is also at the root of the character of Georgian domestic architecture. The conflagration in the capital was fuelled by timber-framed medieval dwellings, but the rebuilding was informed by legislation to prevent the spread of fire from house to house – and this meant building in brick. This legislation culminated in the 1774 London Building Act, and similar building laws were generally adopted in towns and cities throughout the country, as good practice.

Standardization was also encouraged by the increasing publication of pattern books showing how to design and construct houses of all sizes, usually in terraces – both in outline, and in architectural and constructional detail. These design and construction guides, combined with legislation, explain the detailed similarities of Georgian domestic architecture across the land – and it follows that energy efficiency improvements are fittingly similar. Many rural dwellings were also oriented to face south, to take advantage of passive solar gains during winter – a tradition that dates all the way back to the advice of the ancient Roman architect, Vitruvius.

WINDOWS

Although there are some technical problems with elements of Georgian architecture that will impact on potential energy efficiency improvements, windows are not generally one of them. Solid walls are obviously more difficult to thermally upgrade than cavity walls. Georgian roofs are generally complex, with hidden gutters behind parapet walls, combined with valley gutters that can lead to water penetration and dampness; this makes controlled ventilation to roof spaces, and for that matter habitable rooms, of paramount importance. Fortunately, most Georgian houses have high ceiling heights and tall windows, with attractive and eminently functional double-hung sash windows.[1] Incidentally, the invention of the double-hung sash window in the late seventeenth century is generally considered a high point in British architectural development, although some other nations also claim the invention as their own – such as the French.

Georgian windows lose character when glazing bars are lost.

The Invention of the Double-Hung Sash Window

So did the French or the British invent the double-hung sash window? The confusion probably stems from the fact that the French invention of the single-hung sash window (only the bottom frame moves) was probably copied by the British in the mid-seventeenth century. The British architectural breakthrough was to develop the double-hung sash window, in which the top frame also moved. This ingenious invention allows for better ventilation than was possible with either the single-hung or side-hung sash windows. The earliest double-hung sash windows date from around 1700, but by 1720 double-hung sash windows had only spread as far as Holland and the British and Dutch colonies.

The double-hung sash window opens at the top and bottom to aid good ventilation. As hot air rises, cold air generally enters at the bottom, warms up in the room and exhausts through the top opening of the window. Sash windows should be a comfort in times of global warming. The Yorkshire sliding sash operates from side to side – it seems they had to be different to the folks on the other side of the Pennines in Lancashire![2]

Georgian sash windows have narrow glazing bars that help to give the façades their distinctive character – to replace such windows with chunkier modern versions is unthinkable and usually illegal. Also the loss of the original glazing bars severely compromises the character of Georgian houses. Secondary glazing is the only real option to improve the thermal efficiency of Georgian windows – while a 20mm (¾in) air gap is optimal for thermal insulation, a gap of 150mm (6in) is preferable for sound insulation. As many Georgian houses are in urban terraces, somewhere between the two should give a suitable compromise.

Georgian windows usually had internal, wooden shutters that folded back to fit into the often splayed window reveals. Window shutters were a security and privacy feature, and still are, and although many were removed, they should be retained. Such shutters are a useful way to improve window insulation when they are closed at night – almost an old form of double glazing, because the trapped air between the window and the shutter is quite a good thermal (and sound) insulator; furthermore, the shutters can have their thermal efficiency increased with added insulation.

Blind windows are often a feature of Georgian domestic architecture – that is, the outline of a window with reveals, but with no glazed window in place. These are sometimes a conceit to balance the symmetry of the elevation where no window is really needed by the internal plan behind – but they were also a response to the various window taxes that were levied on all but the poorest houses from 1696. The first Window Tax was replaced by another version in 1747, and in 1797 it was trebled to pay for the war with France: this must have brought about an almost overnight reduction in the national number of windows, as they were hastily bricked up and became 'blind'. However, a Brick Tax was also introduced for the same reason in 1794 and 1803 – so as usual, there

was no way to avoid tax, since it was imposed either on the window, or on the bricks that bricked it up! The Brick Tax was finally repealed in 1850, and the Window Tax the following year.

LIGHTING

Georgian town houses are generally well lit by daylight in the principal rooms, usually on the first floor (or *piano nobile*), with their high ceilings and correspondingly tall windows. Well designed artificial lighting schemes, focusing on task and accent lighting, rather than high levels of ambient light, are desirable here. Fanlights above most Georgian entrance doors provide some natural light to hallways, but circulation areas and basements will require more artificial lighting – so energy-efficient light fittings and bulbs are desirable. Legislation already exists in the building regulations to enforce the introduction of energy-efficient lighting where existing lighting systems are being rewired. The European Union will soon completely outlaw tungsten incandescent light bulbs, as these are an inefficient technology that remains unchanged since Thomas Edison invented them a hundred years ago. Ninety per cent of the energy they use is given off as heat, rather than light.

Energy-efficient light bulbs only consume about 20 per cent of the energy of incandescent, tungsten light bulbs, as they predominately create light rather than heat. Halogen bulbs consume less electricity than conventional light bulbs, but more of them are usually needed – so dimmers are a good way to save energy with halogen bulbs. Ranks of halogen downlighters are less than ideal in terms of energy efficiency, and will usually produce a bland ambient lighting feel to spaces. Uplighters generally consume more energy because they use high-wattage bulbs, usually 300 watts or greater (the equivalent of thirty low energy light bulbs) – it is better to use energy-efficient spotlights instead.

Obviously, the best way to save energy is not to use artificial lighting where it is not needed, so switch off lights when rooms are not in use. Most Georgian houses, with their high ceilings and tall windows, should allow for a surfeit of daylight at most times of the year. To evoke the spirit of the Georgian age, when the concept of Romanticism in poetry and literature

Georgian windows with secondary glazing.

Georgian windows with internal shutters.

was born, candle-lit suppers may not go amiss in your efforts to save energy.

A number of myths surround artificial lighting: one is that it is more efficient to leave fluorescent tube light fittings, such as you would use in a kitchen, turned on all the time. This myth has evolved because starting up the tube requires energy – it does need energy, but very little, and if you are going to be out of the room for more than a couple of minutes, then switch them off. Some other issues around electric lighting include the following:

- Electric lighting is responsible for around 15–20 per cent of the average household electricity bill; but with moves to improve insulation, and other measures to reduce space heating bills, this would probably be an increasing proportion.
- Generally, the first thing to do is to replace incandescent tungsten bulbs with low energy compact fluorescent bulbs.
- Turn off the lights when you leave the room.
- Use task lighting, rather than a high level of ambient lighting – good lighting design that uses contrast, such as areas of light and shade, is generally more efficient than increasingly high levels of background light.
- Keep your light bulbs and fixtures clean.
- Rewiring is a good opportunity to overhaul your lighting system and install low energy light fittings and bulbs. All compact fluorescent lights (CFLs) run off mains voltage, and special dimmable versions are available.
- Start installing low energy lighting in areas that are used the most, such as the hall, landings, lounge and kitchen.
- The type of light emitted by a bulb, whether white or yellow – cold or warm – is known as its colour temperature. The lower the temperature, the warmer the light. Early fluorescent lamps had a very cold appearance, but there is now a complete range of temperatures available in low energy lamps.
- Outside security lighting is usually a good area to install low energy bulbs.
- Replacing tungsten bulbs with low energy bulbs has one of the shortest payback periods of any domestic energy efficiency improvement – usually about six months.

- Although low energy light bulbs can cost as much as ten times as much as conventional light bulbs, they last ten times as long on average.
- Low voltage lighting is not necessarily energy efficient – it is the type of bulb and its wattage that is the crucial factor.
- Light-emitting diodes (LEDs) are the potential future of low energy lighting, but they are best used for feature lighting rather than ambient lighting at present. In addition, their use in gardens, stairs and circulation areas is popular. They last a very long time and emit a very small amount of heat.
- Low energy CFLs now come in all shapes and sizes.

HEATING

As in the medieval period, the Georgians had far lower comfort expectations of their dwellings than we do, although there were usually more fireplaces than previously – the Hearth Tax was finally repealed in 1689. But chimneys evolved further to serve multiple fireplaces over a few storeys, and it is important to retain them for aesthetic as well as technical reasons – such as to ensure that traditional solid brick and stone walls have sufficient ventilation to dry out. Some lifestyle compromises are usually necessary to live in a Georgian house.

The architectural history television presenter, Dan Cruickshank, has gone so far as trying to live an authentic Georgian lifestyle in his house in the Spitalfields area of London. He admits that the house is cold, but he wears a hat indoors and his Georgian furniture is designed to take some of the chill off – such as upholstered 'wings' to help insulate him from draughts. Candlelight can also lend the ambience of contrasting light that we often lack in our modern lifestyles! However, there are undoubtedly effective ways to improve the comfort and energy efficiency of Georgian houses in sympathy with their architectural style. Case study 3.2 (see page 64) at the end of this chapter shows the benefits of underfloor heating in the high-ceilinged spaces of most Georgian properties.

CASE STUDIES

Case Study 3.1
A Georgian town house in Bath.

Key points
- Georgian terraced house, listed Grade II.
- Converted into flats.
- Georgian sash windows retained, with concealed draughtproofing.

- Roof uses sealed vapour-permeable construction.
- Lead detailing allows for air paths.
- Basement floor incorporates insulation below stone flags.
- Condensing combination boilers have flues to rear, or in roof valley.
- Mechanical ventilation is humidistat controlled.
- Light pipe to top floor landing and living room.
- Compact fluorescent lamps on stairs controlled by movement sensors and photoelectric cells.

Case Study 3.1 Bath Georgian town house upgrade: rear elevation before refurbishment.

Case Study 3.1 Bath Georgian town house upgrade: rear elevation after refurbishment.

- SAPs raised to between fifty-nine and seventy-five, saving 15 tonnes of carbon dioxide a year.

GENERAL

This case study is a successful demonstration project showing that high levels of energy efficiency can be achieved within the limitations of listed building consent. This Georgian terraced property is typical of Bath and other largely Georgian towns such as Chel-tenham. It has solid walls and single-glazed sash windows, and the basement and rooms in the attic were all uninsulated. The house was already converted into flats when the landlord and Bath City Council instigated a joint project to see how energy efficient they could make this listed property.

Windows

Most of the existing windows are eighteenth-century timber sash windows, subdivided with thin glazing

61

bars. Some were replicas in good condition, but many were original and in poor condition. To replace the area of windows with double glazing was inappropriate, and would have changed irreversibly the character of a historic listed house. The double reflection and thicker glazing bars of modern double glazing would detrimentally alter the appearance of the front façade.

The existing historic windows were therefore overhauled and fitted with concealed draughtproofing. All of the existing internal shutters, which traditionally provide further insulation to the windows when closed, were retained, and replicas added where they were missing.

Walls

The front elevation is of Bath stone, with rubble stone behind and internal timber panelling to the rooms. Although installing insulation by dry-lining the interiors was proposed, this was eventually rejected due to concerns about the 'breathability' of new wall construction and damage to the timber panelling. Insulation was added to the rear wall, which was largely rebuilt.

Floors

Thermal insulation was added to the existing sound insulation between flats, particularly where 'cold bridges' occur, such as where the floors meet the external walls. A 100mm (4in) layer of rigid insulation was installed under the existing basement floors; space for pipes was provided within the layer of new insulation.

Roof

The existing roof was in poor condition, and overhauled. The existing roof covering was taken off, and the timber structure was repaired. New insulation was added to the roof, made out of lambs' wool. Wool insulation is a natural material that is organic and good at absorbing and releasing moisture. The loft was insulated with 200mm (8in) of mineral wool. The ceiling incorporates a vapour barrier, as the new roof space construction does not require ventilation.

Heating

The flats have central heating, with a gas-fired condensing combination boiler. All the gas terminals are at the rear, or hidden in the roof valley for aesthetic reasons. The first floor windows are the largest, due to the proportional system of architectural composition used by the Georgians. On this floor small radiators are positioned underneath the windows to alleviate the cold downdraughts from the single glazing. However, radiators are not positioned underneath the windows on other floors as they might damage the internal timber shutters and panelling. All radiators have thermostatic radiator valves (TRVs).

The heating is controlled by a seven-day programmable thermostat with a remote sensor. Radio links from the boilers to the thermosats were used in some areas to avoid damaging building fabric with wires.

Ventilation

Background ventilation is from vents in the existing fireplaces, and the sash windows can be opened slightly, if required. Energy-efficient fans provide extract ventilation in the kitchens and bathrooms – the terminals are hidden in the roof valleys. Recirculating hoods are used over most cookers.

Lighting

The interior walls and floor finishes are light, off-white, traditional colours to maximize the reflection of daylight and electric light. Two large-diameter sunpipes were installed on the top floor to increase natural lighting; they are a more energy-efficient option than roof lights in this situation. The electric lighting consists of energy-efficient lamps and multiple switches to control artificial lighting levels. All light fittings are designed to take compact fluorescent lamps (CFL). The communal staircase and entrance hall share a sophisticated lighting system that incorporates normal, emergency and night-time background lighting into each fitting. This is controlled by a combination of movement sensors and photo-electric cells, and uses CFLs with high frequency dimmable ballasts. The front and rear area lights are controlled by movement sensors.

Energy Ratings

Unimproved SAP ratings were generally one. The SAP ratings achieved for the completed work vary from fifty-nine to seventy-nine, depending on the position of the flat in the building. This represents an annual saving of approximately 15 tonnes of carbon dioxide per year for the whole building. U values are: roof 0.17 Wm^2K / mansard 0.38 Wm^2K; lowest floor 0.22 Wm^2K / upper floors 0.29 Wm^2K.

Recycled Materials

Existing items were repaired rather than replaced wherever possible. Roof tiles were secondhand. Stone flags were reused internally and externally. New stone was taken from a local quarry.

Water Conservation

All water supplies are metered. Showers are provided in all flats.

Note: Replacing the windows, rather than repairing and draughtproofing them, would have needed listed building consent. Moreover, replacement would have resulted in the loss of irreplaceable original fabric. It is important to remember that it is a criminal offence to carry out, or to cause unauthorized works to a listed building. The Listed Buildings Act 1990 has provisions for fines up to £20,000, and six months imprisonment. Case law records fines of up to £75,000.

Georgian terraced house in Edinburgh.

Case Study 3.2

Georgian terraced housing in Edinburgh.

Key points

- Converted into flats.
- Underfloor heating installed.
- Condensing boilers installed.
- Roof insulation installed.

General

Much Georgian housing in town and city centres is now subdivided into flats, or very often changed in use to offices – or to other uses, for that matter. Underfloor heating is generally more suitable for rooms with high ceilings as it provides a more even temperature gradient from floor to ceiling. As with medieval houses, natural insulation materials, such as sheep's wool, are more appropriate for Georgian roof spaces.

Heating

Underfloor heating systems have become popular recently; they are usually suitable for Georgian houses, and do away with the need for radiators. Obviously, such an overhaul in a heating system is best done when major renovation work is planned. As underfloor heating introduces heat at a lower level than radiators, it should also give improved comfort conditions and lower running costs. It operates at lower water-flow temperatures than conventional radiator systems, which makes it particularly suitable for condensing boilers, as their efficiency is optimized at low flow temperatures.

A high-ceilinged Georgian room can produce temperature stratification, with all the hot air collecting near the ceiling, rather than providing heating comfort for occupants – this usually leads to excessive amounts of energy being used to adequately heat such rooms. Underfloor heating does not produce such temperature stratification, and usually requires boiler sizes of about half that of conventional systems, all of which leads to savings in both capital and running costs, and in energy. In the recent renovation of a flat on two storeys in a former Georgian house in Edinburgh, capital savings were made of several thousand pounds over a conventional heating system, and several hundred pounds a year in running costs.

SUMMARY

- Georgian architecture is inspired by Roman and Greek classical architecture in appearance and proportions. Neo-classical architecture was interpreted by Italian Renaissance architects such as Andrea Palladio (1508–80), and British architects such as Sir Christopher Wren (1632–1723).
- Many of the crescents, squares and terraced streets in central London, and towns such as Bath and Bristol, date from the Georgian era.
- Most Georgian houses, in towns and cities at least, were speculatively built, but are now sought-after properties, often listed, or in conservation areas.
- After the Fire of London in 1666, similar building laws were generally adopted in towns and cities throughout the country. Standardization explains the detailed similarities of Georgian domestic architecture – and it follows that energy efficiency improvements are fittingly similar.
- Most Georgian houses have rooms with high ceilings and tall windows, with attractive and eminently functional sash windows. The invention of the sash window was a high point in British architectural development.
- Georgian sash windows have narrow glazing bars that help to give the Georgian façade its distinctive character – to replace such windows with a chunkier modern version is unthinkable and usually illegal. Secondary glazing is an option, with a 20mm (¾in) air gap as optimal for thermal insulation, and a gap of 150mm (6in) ideal for sound insulation.
- Georgian windows usually had internal wooden shutters: these are a useful way to improve window insulation when they are closed at night, and they can even have their thermal efficiency increased with added insulation.
- Electric lighting is responsible for around 15–20 per cent of the average household light bill; with moves to improve insulation, and other measures to reduce space heating bills, this could probably become an increasing proportion.
- Energy-efficient light bulbs only consume about 20 per cent of the energy of incandescent, tungsten light bulbs, as they predominately create light rather than heat.

- Rewiring is a good opportunity to overhaul your lighting system and install low energy light fittings and bulbs. All compact fluorescent lights (CFLs) run off mains voltage, and special dimmable versions are available.
- Replacing tungsten bulbs with low energy bulbs usually pays back in about six months. Although low energy light bulbs can cost as much as ten times more than conventional light bulbs, they last ten times as long on average.
- High-ceilinged Georgian rooms can produce temperature stratification, with all the hot air collecting near the ceiling, rather than providing heating comfort for occupants. Underfloor heating does not produce such temperature stratification, and usually requires boiler sizes of about half that of conventional systems.
- Dan Cruickshank lives an authentic Georgian lifestyle in his house in Spitalfields, London. Although the house is cold, he wears a hat indoors and his Georgian furniture has upholstered 'wings' to help insulate him from draughts.

CHAPTER 4

Victorian: 1837–1901

OVERVIEW

From 1800–1900 the population of Great Britain quadrupled, from 10 million to 40 million people. This historically unprecedented population growth was sustained by the prosperity of advanced industrialization and urbanization, not to mention the far global reach of the British Empire. On the eve of World War I, 80 per cent of England's population lived in cities, as compared with a 40 per cent urban population when Queen Victoria ascended the throne in 1837. Dense urbanization was possible through the spatial efficiency of terraced housing, from the humble two-up, two-down, back-to-back typologies in town and city centres, through to the burgeoning suburbs.

The Victorian terraced house is inherently a model of sustainable development in terms of compactness, interconnection, mixed use and affordability. Recent studies of sustainable housing forms recommend close study of Victorian estates, and adaptation of their layout principles to contemporary development. The architectural form of the Victorian terrace is still regularly reinterpreted in modern housing developments. About a third of Britain's dwellings were erected between 1800 and 1911 (several million houses), and a third of them between 1870 and 1911. Traditional domestic construction techniques did not change significantly over the period 1837–1919, apart from obvious improvements due to improved building regulations, sanitation and local by-laws.

Dramatic urbanization throughout the nineteenth century means that the majority of surviving Victorian housing is concentrated in large conurbations such as London, Birmingham, Manchester, Liverpool and Bristol. However, the notion of suburbs of villas was implemented in St Johns Wood, London, in 1820. Although speculatively built, this suburb of detached villas in their own grounds provided the usually unobtainable ideal of domesticity well into the Victorian era. But the burgeoning Victorian middle classes led the way with terraces of semi-detached villas on the edge of towns, while more prosaic terraces housed the urban population influx. Much of the capital for small housing was invested by the middle classes, as property gave a return slightly better than government stocks and slightly less than more risky ventures such as railways – thus the term 'as safe as houses' was coined. Paradoxically, the majority of the population rented their dwellings, with only about 10 per cent as owner-occupiers, compared to around 70 per cent today.

Stylistically, Victorian architecture is famous, or infamous, for its eclecticism. The neo-classical architectural influences of the Georgian period spilled over into a classical revival – or more particularly a revival of ancient Greek architecture. Classical architecture was pitted against the exponents of Gothic revival architecture, but this battle of the styles was largely played out in the arena of public and institutional buildings, rather than houses. The Gothic style did not lend itself to small-scale domesticity, nor for that matter did Greek architecture – although public buildings such as the Houses of Parliament and the Law Courts in the Strand are famous examples of the former; while The National Gallery in Trafalgar Square and the quadrangle and portico of University College London are good examples of the latter.

Typical Victorian semi-detached houses, Cambridge.

Typical Victorian terraced housing, North London.

Typical Victorian terraced housing, Watford.

Typical Victorian semi-detached villas, North London.

Victorian terraced housing in Edinburgh.

An Italianate villa style became the main inspiration for early Victorian domestic architecture. Later in Victoria's reign, the revival of English vernacular architectural styles and the Arts and Crafts Movement dictated the appearance of suburbia well into the twentieth century. In many suburbs of London, and in other towns and cities throughout the country, late nineteenth-century housing predominates, usually consisting of two-storey terraces with large bay windows. Ultimately, Victorian suburban housing became as uniform as that of the Georgian era, as mass production and the cheap transport of the railways made similar building materials, such as bricks, ubiquitous across the land, where once local materials had dominated.

BUILDING CONSERVATION

Many nineteenth-century dwellings are handsome examples of mid-Victorian, solid stone, bay-windowed terraces, of heritage value in their own right. The majority are more architecturally mediocre, but their value in terms of context and streetscape should not be underestimated. A strong economic argument for conservation is tourism, in that an attractive historic environment which attracts tourists depends not only on the few 'Great Sights', but also on scenic variety – a sense that a place is different and, above all, old.

Tourists see in British domestic architecture qualities that many locals take for granted – until they lose them. Seemingly humble examples of British domestic architecture would be given listed status if they

The Orchard, Chorleywood, Hertfordshire by Charles Voysey, 1899.

Terraced housing in Middle Road, Harrow-on-the-Hill, by Edward S. Prior, 1887.

were sited in the New World. Many foreign architects and planners still visit Britain to study housing from the Victorian era, as they have done for the past hundred years. There was a period from the 1940s to the 1970s when some professionals condemned the suburban row house and advocated other types of dwelling, such as high-rise blocks. But social problems with high-rise living, and the Ronan Point collapse, contributed to the eclipse of such housing solutions and the return to favour of the terrace, which forms so much of Victorian housing.

The large amount of Victorian housing that has survived has done so not just because it is flexible, but because it is popular with the general public. They still approve of, and can afford, the legacy of terraced and other Victorian housing. Such housing fulfils today's demands in almost all respects: the small- to medium-sized, two-storey, three bedroomed family house, with upstairs bathroom and WC, with full drainage and other modern conveniences (even central heating, usually installed in the 1960s), and a private garden at the back. Although the plan of two-up, two-down rooms and layouts are similar, strong traditions of local building and materials continued until late in the nineteenth century; it was only in the early twentieth century that brick-making became a national industry, and regional production petered out.

The construction quality of Victorian housing was not immune from bad workmanship, but the stock that has survived for well over a hundred years must be the best. No age is free from construction mistakes, but at the end of the nineteenth century there were frequent comments about improved construction, even in small houses. Building regulations and local by-laws did not eradicate bad construction, but they seemed to reduce the scope for it.

In terms of materials, Portland cement (patented in 1824) was universally used for all foundations and drainage pipe joints by the late nineteenth century. Damp-proof courses were introduced from around 1850 from 1890 all new housing in Manchester used them, and by 1900 new buildings almost invariably included them. From the 1860s–1870s onwards, floorboards were no longer permitted to lie on the ground, even in small houses, heralding ubiquitous perforated 'air bricks' to ventilate suspended floors – ideal for energy-efficient upgrading with insulation.

Conservation not only preserves cultural values, it is also ecologically friendly as it preserves a large investment in energy, materials and skills. It also adds value and prestige to large central areas, and strengthens social ties among local residents. The refurbishment of historic housing stock also provides opportunities for training craftspeople in traditional building and conservation techniques – work that constitutes about half of the construction work undertaken annually.

The surviving stock of Victorian housing has already implicitly demonstrated its ability to adapt to changing social and technical needs – there are countless examples of Victorian housing reversibly converted into multi-residential units, demonstrating its inherent flexibility.

ENERGY CONSERVATION

There are also many examples of Victorian terraced housing that are refurbished to high standards of energy efficiency. The refurbishment of solid-walled houses can achieve SAP ratings equal to, or better than those of new-build properties complying with building regulations (Standard Assessment Procedure – the government's standard method of home energy rating).[1] The energy-efficient measures generally most cost-effective in Victorian, solid-walled houses are:

- loft insulation;
- insulated dry lining to external walls – or external insulating render;
- ground floor insulation;
- secondary glazing;
- gas central heating with condensing boiler;
- factory-insulated hot water cylinder;
- controlled ventilation system.

Other non-energy benefits include:

- reduced maintenance costs due to fewer condensation problems;
- higher property value or rental income;
- management costs savings.

In addition, and ironically, many Victorian houses, particularly in rural locations, included features such as basement cisterns for the storage of rainwater – a practical measure before the advent of mains water supplies to rural locations. Such practical historic features are now being reinvented in the name of environmental sustainability – what goes around, comes around.

ROOF SPACES – INSULATION IMPROVEMENTS

Around two-thirds of domestic energy use is usually for space heating. Heat rises, and the roof is the part of the house most exposed to the weather, so it follows that insulating the loft is a good starting point to improve the performance of a Victorian house. Such measures can reduce space heating costs by about 20 per cent, and even more if there is no existing insulation. The optimum depth for roof insulation is 250–300mm (10–12in). Even in Victorian houses that already have some loft insulation, this is likely to be between the ceiling joists and only 100mm (4in) or so deep – topping up the insulation to 300mm (12in) in such cases is well worthwhile. The payback period of such an investment, if there is no roof insulation, is around a year. Even if there is 50mm (2in) of insulation in the roof, the payback period of topping up to 300mm is only about four to five years.

Additional roof insulation also has the benefit of reducing solar heat gains in summer – particularly as we move towards higher temperatures brought about by global warming and climate change. However, insulating the loft space is the relatively easy option where ventilation to the roof space must be maintained, usually with eaves ventilators. Other issues include the need for a boarded access path to get to the water tank, where the insulation covers ceiling joists; and the insulation of water tanks to prevent them freezing in a colder attic. Using a natural insulation material such as sheep's wool means that slightly less thickness is needed, and it is easier to work with than mineral wool/fibre materials. Insulation improvements to Victorian roof spaces that are converted into an attic room or room in the roof are technically trickier.

Room in the Roof – Insulation Improvements

Insulation improvements at rafter level to a pitched Victorian roof are more complicated than improving insulation at ceiling level. Although such upgrades are practical at any time, they are most cost-effective when the loft is being converted into a habitable

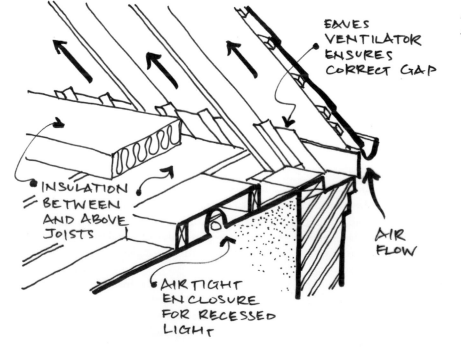

Roof insulation to loft space.

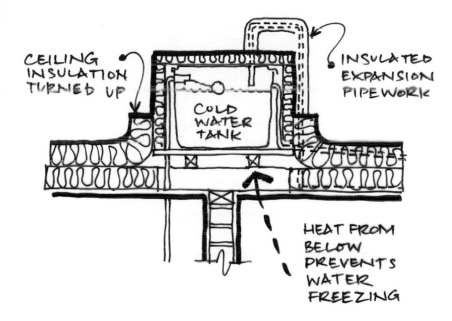

CEILING
INSULATION
TURNED UP

INSULATED
EXPANSION
PIPEWORK

COLD
WATER
TANK

HEAT FROM
BELOW
PREVENTS
WATER
FREEZING

Cold water tank insulation.

space, or when the roof covering is being replaced. If the roof covering has reached the end of its life and it is time to replace it with new tiles, this also presents the opportunity to insulate the roof at rafter level to create what is known technically as a 'warm roof'.

A warm roof is created when rigid insulation is placed above the roof structure – usually rafters and purlins in a Victorian roof. The term 'warm roof' refers to the fact that the structure is on the warm side of the insulation. Opting for a warm roof insulation improvement means that there is no need for ventilation or a vapour control barrier, as there is no 'thermal bridge' to create a cold surface for condensation. However, this kind of improvement should generally be undertaken by a specialist. The warm roof insulation upgrade is not always possible due to the fact that it slightly raises the height of the roof ridge by the thickness of the rigid insulation that is installed – which is rather impractical and unsightly if applied to one Victorian house in a terrace. Such alterations to listed buildings and houses in conservation areas are unlikely to meet with listed building consent or planning approval. The alternative of adding insulation underneath or between the roof rafters is the best option in these cases, creating what is known as a 'cold roof'.

The cold roof insulation upgrade requires roof ven-

tilation from one eaves to the other, and also at the ridge for roof pitches over 35 degrees. A vapour control layer is also required, usually behind the raking plasterboard lining of the room-in-the-roof ceiling. Headroom in the attic room is sometimes an issue with this type of insulation upgrade, but there are insulation products as thin as 20–25mm (¾–1in) that have good U-values, if headroom is at a premium. If it is not so crucial, it may be possible to place insulation in between the rafters as well as underneath them, so that the rafter no longer acts as a thermal bridge. But when placing insulation between rafters, a ventilation space of at least 50mm (2in) should be left above the insulation.

Interstitial condensation, which is condensation between or within the layers of the roof construction, is risked if inadequate ventilation is provided, or if the vapour control layer is placed in the wrong position. Interstitial condensation may still occur in the cold roof upgrade to a traditional Victorian building, as the roof structure still needs to breathe – and the introduction of an impervious, vapour control layer (for example, a polythene sheet) is more appropriate for modern houses. For a Victorian house, it is more appropriate to use a vapour check of much lower vapour resistance than a polythene membrane, such as a modern 'breather' membrane.

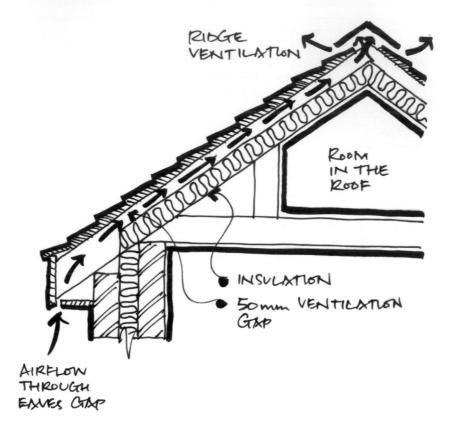

Roof insulation to attic room – cold roof construction.

RIDGE
VENTILATION

ROOM
IN THE
ROOF

INSULATION

50mm VENTILATION
GAP

AIRFLOW
THROUGH
EAVES GAP

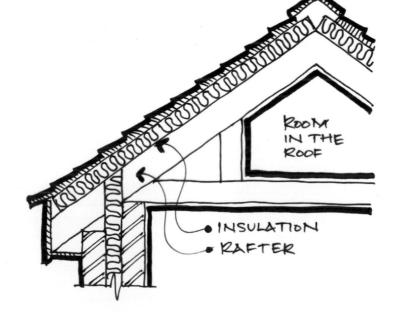

Roof insulation to attic room – warm roof construction.

ROOM
IN THE
ROOF

INSULATION

RAFTER

74

CASE STUDIES

Case Study 4.1

Two mid-Victorian terraced houses in Cambridge.

Key Points

- Renovation of two adjacent Victorian houses, combined and extended.
- Use of natural materials with low-embodied energy.
- Natural daylight and ventilation improved.
- Triple-glazed, argon-filled windows installed.
- Internal insulation added to solid brick walls.
- Insulated ground floor and underfloor heating installed.
- High efficiency gas condensing boiler installed.
- Natural passive stack ventilation system installed.
- Low-water usage appliances installed.
- Air-tightness testing undertaken.

General

An expanding family living in a Victorian terraced house in Cambridge acquired their neighbour's house when it came up for sale, rather than move to a larger house. This provided the opportunity for an environmentally friendly refurbishment of the two adjacent houses into a spacious abode for a larger family. The brief required the conversion of the two mid-Victorian houses into a five-bedroom house with ancillary accommodation, including the use of loft space and a large lounge. Energy efficiency was a prerequisite within the wider context of creating a

Case Study 4.1 Cambridge terraced houses – front elevation.

Case Study 4.1 Cambridge terraced houses – garden elevation.

refurbished house to overall environmental best practice. Natural materials were specified, such as natural and organic paints, waxes and stains.

Windows

The Victorian sash windows to the front bay windows and above were replaced with double-glazed and draught-stripped timber windows in the original Victorian style. Insulation was added to the roofs and side walls of the bay windows when the windows were replaced – there is even an insulated and airtight cat flap! The new windows to the rear and sides of the property are triple glazed, with low emissivity glass, and argon fill and insulated spacer bars give a U-value of $1.0W/m^2K$.

Walls

The solid brick walls of the terraced houses were thermally improved by dry-lining them with 100mm

(4in) of insulation. The existing kitchen extension contained a cavity wall filled with 100mm of insulation, and 100mm of dry-lined insulation was also added.

Floors

The existing timber suspended floor on the ground floor was replaced with a solid floor, with underfloor, low temperature heating and 200mm (8in) of insulation underneath. A damp-proof membrane was also installed. Thermal bridging was reduced by careful detailing at the edge of the floor slab.

Roof

The attic space, used as a study and spare room with en suite, had restricted headroom, so 200mm (8in) of insulation was added between the rafters. Thermal bridging was minimized by careful detailing, such as adding a further 25mm (1in) of insulation to the underside of the rafters with a plasterboard lining and counter battens.

Heating

The low temperature water circulation required for the ground floor underfloor heating is ideal for the new, high efficiency, gas condensing boiler that was installed. Radiators were installed upstairs. A wood-burning stove was positioned in the centre of the house. Room thermostats, radiators with thermostatic radiator valves (TRVs) and weather compensation controls were also installed.

Ventilation

The building achieved five air changes per hour in an air-tightness test (the average in UK housing is around thirteen). As the building fabric did not contain materials that were particularly sensitive, a ventilation system was installed, a natural passive stack ventilation with humidity controls.

Lighting

Windows were provided to all habitable rooms, and rooflights were included in the filled-in space between the backs of the two houses: this space became the new dining room. Natural finishes, such as a slate floor and earth-plaster walls, give this space the feeling of a conservatory. Low energy light fittings are used throughout, together with low energy appliances (A-rated white goods).

Case Study 4.2

The Nottingham eco-home.

Key Points

- Late Victorian semi-detached house, dating from 1898.
- Converted into an energy-efficient eco-home.
- Triple-glazed French windows to the north façade, krypton-filled with two low emissivity coatings.
- Thermally lined fabric blinds increase night-time insulation to windows.
- Super-insulation to roof space and breather membrane added.
- External and internal insulation added to solid brick walls.

- Heat recovery fans installed in kitchen and bathrooms.
- Solar water-heating panel added to roof.
- Insulation added to floors.
- Wood burning boiler installed in the cellar.
- Energy costs were reduced by 75 per cent, saving 16 tonnes of carbon dioxide a year.

General

This case study shows how a typical late Victorian, solid-walled dwelling can be effectively refurbished – most of the savings come from more efficient building fabric, heating and hot water. The property in Nottingham was completely refurbished over several years by the broadcaster Penney Poyzer and architect Gil Schalom. The house, dating from 1898, was somewhat dilapidated after being used for student housing for a few decades. The new owners approached the refurbishment with five basic principles in mind, applicable to all old houses, when retrofitting their house:

- Super-insulation – to add as much thermal insulation as possible.
- Passive solar design – to optimize the large bay windows to the entrance façade, as they are south facing and benefit from solar warmth, especially in winter.
- Thermal mass – to capitalize on the ability of solid materials such as brickwork to store heat and then release it when it becomes cooler. For example, the solid stone walls of a cathedral are able to store thermal energy on a hot day so that the interior remains comfortably cool for occupants.
- Air-tightness and controlled ventilation – to improve, as most old houses are quite draughty due to air gaps in their construction, such as around windows and doors.
- Thermal bridging – to rationalize, as older construction details using solid brick walls, stone lintels over windows and solid floors often create thermal bridges to the outside, which increase heat losses from the interior.

The owners were also keen to show their environmental credentials, and went beyond energy efficiency to embrace wider issues of environmental sustainability. These include harvesting rainwater, a

Case Study 4.2 Nottingham eco-home – front elevation.

hybrid composting lavatory, and using natural materials such as sheep's wool for insulation.

Windows

The original single-glazed sash windows had been replaced with double-glazed u-PVC windows by the previous owner. It was decided to replace these with more environmentally sustainable, timber-framed, high performance double-glazed windows as and when they failed. Two new sets of French windows were installed to the north, garden façade – these were triple glazed, filled with krypton gas and coated with two coats of low emissivity coating. Filling a double- or triple-glazing unit with inert gas such as argon or krypton provides higher insulation than air, while a

low emissivity coating to the inside of the glass reflects heat back into the room. These can economically improve the thermal performance of the windows by around two-thirds.

Walls

The external walls of the house were 225mm (9in) thick solid brickwork, typical of Victorian house construction. Cavity walls did not become common in domestic building until after the 1920s. External insulation of 140mm (5½in) expanded polystyrene covered with a render system was installed, which significantly improved the thermal performance of the walls. Internal insulation was installed to the south, entrance elevation so that the external appearance of brickwork was retained – this dry-lining took the form of two layers of 50mm (2in) closed cell insulation laminate boards.

Floors

Areas of the ground floor solid floor were excavated to place new damp-proof membranes (dpm). Also 150mm (6in) of polystyrene insulation was placed, with 50mm (2in) edge upstands to prevent cold bridging, under a new 100mm (4in) concrete slab. Polystyrene is one of the cheapest insulating materials, and although not biodegradable, it is one of the few materials suitable for under-slab solid floor construction. Areas of the suspended timber ground floor were filled with 100mm sheep's wool between joists. At first floor level the existing floorboards were taken up and the joists strengthened – loose rockwool insulation was placed between joists to provide sound insulation.

Roof

The roof space was super-insulated with 300mm (12in) of blown recycled newspaper insulation contained in a plywood web between rafters, and 400mm (16in) of recycled newspaper insulation above and between ceiling joists. The roof had been built without roofing felt under the tiling battens, and had functioned adequately for a century like that. The decision to rebuild the roof covering, recycling most of the roofing tiles, allowed a geotextile breather membrane to be inserted, to protect the new insulation. Breather membrane is impervious to water but allows water vapour, such as condensation, to escape from inside the roof. The overhang of the roof eaves was also increased to protect the new external insulation.

Heating

A wood-burning boiler was installed in the cellar for central heating and hot water top-up, but 4sq m (45sq ft) of flat-plate solar panel on the south-facing roof pitch caters for half of the hot water demand.

Ventilation

Ventilation in older houses becomes crucial once energy efficiency improvements are made. Historic building construction is invariably draughty, which, while potentially uncomfortable for inhabitants, also allows moisture to escape from inside the house – it allows the old house to 'breathe', so that typically solid wall construction dries out after absorbing moisture from rainfall, inhabitants and their activities. Reducing ventilation in old houses and making them more airtight and comfortable inevitably causes problems of condensation in wet areas such as bathrooms and kitchens.

As conventional extractor fans also extract heat, heat recovery fans, which save up to 80 per cent of airborne heat, were installed in bathrooms and both kitchens. A 'whole house' mechanical heat recovery system was also installed.

Energy Ratings

Overall energy costs were reduced from approximately £3,500 (original specification before the u-PVC windows were installed) to around £900 per year. This saving of around 75 per cent of energy costs translates into an 85 per cent saving of carbon dioxide emissions – from 19 tonnes to 3 tonnes per year. The majority of savings come from the reduction in heating requirements enjoyed because of the insulation improvements to the building fabric (a saving of 13 tonnes of carbon dioxide per year). Energy-efficient hot water provision accounts for a further saving of 2.5 tonnes of carbon dioxide per year. The U-values of the house's fabric were improved as follows:

- Roof: from 1.9 to 0.12 Wm^2K
- Ground floor: from 0.7 to 0.2 Wm^2K
- Walls: from 2.1 to 0.2 Wm^2K
- Windows: from 4.7 to 1.5 Wm^2K

Water Conservation

Rainwater is harvested from the roof and stored in two tanks in the cellar; these have a total capacity of 2,000ltr (440gal). This is reminiscent of water cisterns that were installed in the cellars of Victorian houses, at least in rural areas. Copper was specified for new gutters and rainwater downpipes, as it does not rust and has a mild disinfecting effect on the water. The filtered rainwater is used to flush toilets and supply the washing machine and a garden tap. Rainwater collection saves about half of mains water requirements.

Ideally, a composting lavatory would have been installed to maximize water savings, but the compromise of a hybrid system was selected for ease of resale.

The hybrid lavatory has a water-flushing system with a composting system to deal with solid waste.

Case Study 4.3
Collymore Cottages.

Key Points
- Late Victorian rural house owned by the National Trust.
- Interior insulation installed without adding moisture membranes.
- Careful detailing to internal features, such as architraves.
- Carbon dioxide savings of 2.8 tonnes for each house.

General

These National Trust cottages are good examples of typical Victorian rural houses. They do not have a damp-proof course (dpc) in their solid brick walls, or a damp-proof membrane (dpm) under the ground floor. As such, like all traditionally constructed houses, they rely on evaporation from effective ventilation rates to remain dry. Many modern methods of insulation improvements by internal dry-lining include vapour checks that are inappropriate to traditional forms of construction. The inclusion of a modern vapour check, such as polythene sheet, to the interior dry-lining of Victorian houses risks interstitial condensation. Trapped water vapour diffuses through layers of materials until it meets a cold surface where

Case Study 4.3 Collymore Cottages – external view.

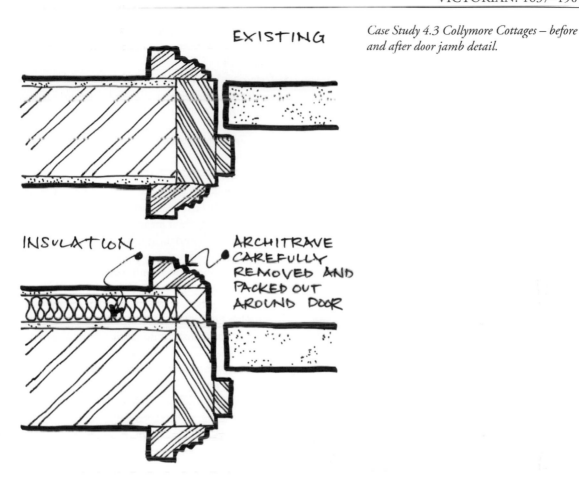

EXISTING

INSULATION

ARCHITRAVE CAREFULLY REMOVED AND PACKED OUT AROUND DOOR

Case Study 4.3 Collymore Cottages – before and after door jamb detail.

it condenses – in the middle of the building fabric. There is a particular risk of interstitial condensation when adding insulation to the inside, or heated side of the structure. Professional advice and calculation methods are often necessary to ensure that proposals will not result in interstitial condensation. Traditional house construction needs to 'breathe'.

The calculations showed that if a typical dry-lining material such as polystyrene were added to Collymore Cottages, it would prevent moisture being able to evaporate from the inner surface of the walls. A mineral wool-backed board, without a built-in vapour check, was used instead. A coat of internal mineral paint was applied to the board to give it just the right amount of vapour resistance to avoid the risk of interstitial condensation, without compromising the ability of the house's traditional construction to breathe. This is known as a low vapour-resistance solution.

Internal dry-lining to old houses requires careful thought and detailing.

SUMMARY

- From 1800–1900 the population of Great Britain quadrupled, from 10 million to 40 million people. On the eve of World War I, 80 per cent of England's population lived in cities, as compared with a 40 per cent urban population when Queen Victoria ascended the throne in 1837.
- Dense urbanization was possible through the spatial efficiency of terraced housing, from the humble two-up, two-down, back-to-back typologies in town and city centres, through to the burgeoning suburbs.
- The Victorian terraced house is inherently a model of sustainable development in terms of

compactness, interconnection, mixed use and affordability. Recent studies of sustainable housing forms recommend close study of Victorian estates, and adaptation of their layout principles to contemporary development.

- About a third of Britain's dwellings were erected between 1800 and 1911 (several million houses), and a third of them between 1870 and 1911. Traditional domestic construction techniques did not change significantly over the period 1837–1919, apart from obvious improvements due to improved building regulations, sanitation and local by-laws.

- Victorian architecture is famous, or infamous, for its eclectic style. Classical architecture was pitted against the exponents of Gothic revival architecture. The National Gallery in Trafalgar Square and University College London are good examples of the former – while the Houses of Parliament and the Law Courts in the Strand are famous examples of the latter.

- An Italianate villa style became the main inspiration for early Victorian domestic architecture. Later in Victoria's reign, the revival of English vernacular architectural styles and the Arts and Crafts Movement dictated the appearance of suburbia well into the twentieth century – usually consisting of two-storey terraces with large bay windows.

- Ultimately, Victorian suburban housing became as uniform as that of the Georgian era, as mass-produced materials, such as bricks, replaced local ones, with the coming of the railways.

- Many foreign architects and planners still visit Britain to study housing from the Victorian era. The Victorian terraced house has largely returned to favour, after experiments in modern housing types such as the high-rise block.

- The construction quality of Victorian housing was not immune from bad workmanship, but at the end of the nineteenth century there were frequent comments about improved construction, even in small houses. Damp-proof courses were introduced from around 1850, and by 1900 new buildings almost invariably included them. Floorboards were no longer permitted to lie on the ground, even in small houses, from the 1860s–1870s onwards, heralding ubiquitous perforated 'air bricks' to ventilate suspended floors – ideal for energy-efficient upgrading with insulation.

- Conservation not only preserves cultural values, it is also ecologically friendly as it preserves a large investment in energy, materials and skills. The surviving stock of Victorian housing has already implicitly demonstrated its ability to adapt to changing social and technical needs – it is inherently flexible. There are countless examples of Victorian housing reversibly converted into multi-residential units, demonstrating their flexibility.

- The energy-efficient measures generally most cost-effective in Victorian, solid-walled houses are loft insulation; insulated dry-lining to external walls – or external insulating render; ground floor insulation; secondary glazing; gas central heating with condensing boiler; factory-insulated hot water cylinder; controlled ventilation system.

- Around two-thirds of domestic energy use is usually for space heating. Insulating the loft is a good starting point to improve the performance of a Victorian house. Such measures can reduce space heating costs by about 20 per cent, and even more if there is no existing insulation. The optimum depth for roof insulation is 250–300mm (10–12in).

- Five basic principles to keep in mind when improving a Victorian house are super-insulation; passive solar design; thermal mass; air-tightness; and thermal bridging.

- Many modern methods of insulation improvements include vapour checks that are inappropriate to traditional forms of construction. The inclusion of a modern vapour check, such as polythene sheet, to Victorian houses risks interstitial condensation. Trapped water vapour diffuses through layers of materials until it meets a cold surface where it condenses – in the middle of the building fabric. There is a particular risk of interstitial condensation when adding insulation to the inside, or heated side of the structure. Professional advice and calculation methods are often necessary to ensure that proposals will not result in interstitial condensation. Traditional house construction needs to 'breathe'.

CHAPTER 5

Edwardian: 1901–1914

OVERVIEW

The Edwardian period is generally associated with the height of the British Empire, and although George V ascended to the throne in 1910, it effectively lasted until the beginning of World War I in 1914. The turn of the nineteenth into the twentieth century heralded many social and technological changes, not least of which were in domestic architecture. The difference in attitudes between the comic character of Mr Charles Pooter and his son Lupin provides an amusing contrast between the stereotypical late Victorian

patriarch, and the next middle-class generation – the Edwardians.[1] If anyone ever applies the term 'Pooterish' to your behaviour, you will know that you were petty and pedantic – unless of course it refers to your attempts to reduce your carbon footprint, and bring your Edwardian house into line with the energy consumption of a modern energy-efficient abode! Edwardian domestic architecture bridges the gap between late Victorian suburbs and the speculative housing styles of inter-war suburbia.

The railways were further expanding and allowing

Typical Edwardian semi-detached houses, London.

Hollybank, Chorleywood, Hertfordshire by Charles Voysey, 1904.

Typical stained glass in an Edwardian house.

Rural Edwardian semi-detached houses in Hertfordshire.

longer commuter journeys from suburbia to town and city centres, typified by Metro-land in the Home Counties to the north-west of London. The Edwardian semi-detached house became the norm for middle-class housing, largely inspired by the Arts and Crafts Movement. The artistic house lay at the stylistic roots of Edwardian suburban developments, with its emphasis on health, sanitation, fresh air and light. Victorian domestic interiors were typically dark, whereas Edwardian ones were light and bright in colour. There were pragmatic reasons for this change in taste, as light interiors were impractical in an age of soot from candles and paraffin and gas lamps. And gas lighting remained a middle-class luxury until well into the Edwardian era.[2]

The dawn of domestic electric lighting was, however, reaching middle-class suburbs in the Edwardian period, and it allowed a new outlook in terms of interior design. In 1909 it was calculated that a room covered in brown oak panelling or maroon paint would

need almost three times the candle power than that of the same room with a white ceiling and cream walls. But the new electric light was weak, and the most popular lamp was equivalent to the light of sixteen candles, or to a modern 25-watt incandescent tungsten bulb.[3] Electric light quickly became a status symbol, and the harbinger of a more profligate age in terms of the use of energy in general. Other labour-saving devices, such as the electric kettle and the electric clothes iron, were quick to follow – to the extent that we each now use several times the energy that a typical Edwardian did.

ENERGY EFFICIENCY

The Energy Saving Trust estimates that a typical Edwardian house, built in around 1910, is emitting 8 tonnes of carbon dioxide every year, compared to 5 tonnes emitted by a typical house built in the mid-1970s, and 4 tonnes from new housing built after the

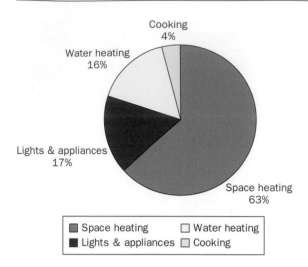

Cooking
4%

Water heating
16%

Lights & appliances
17%

Space heating
63%

■ Space heating   □ Water heating
■ Lights & appliances   ▢ Cooking

*Typical energy use in an unimproved
Edwardian house.*

mid-1990s. The typical, unimproved Edwardian house is emitting twice the CO_2 per year of a modern house because of its typical original features, such as solid walls, bay or sash windows with single glazing, and open fireplaces; this also means that such an unimproved Edwardian house is using nearly two-thirds of its energy on space heating. Furthermore the improvement of thermal insulation and space-heating energy efficiency is also typically the most cost-effective way to begin improving the performance of an Edwardian house.

Although modest energy efficiency improvements were usually made, over the decades, to Edwardian housing – such as 50–100mm (2–4in) loft insulation, new boiler and radiators, double glazing, draught-proofing and some low energy lighting – these measures will not bring the house up to current standards, and more improvements are required to do this, such as:

- adding more loft insulation – up to 250–300mm (10–12in);
- adding a new condensing boiler;
- improving the heating and hot water controls;
- adding a well insulated hot water cylinder;
- insulating the solid walls;
- installing low-energy lighting;
- choosing appliances that are energy efficient.[4]

SOLID WALLS

Clearly the only way to improve the thermal conductive properties of a solid wall is to add insulation on the inside or the outside. Usually the way to improve the insulation of solid walls with the least technical risk is to add insulation to the outside – creating a 'warm wall' that largely avoids cold or thermal bridging. This has the added advantage that the thermal mass of the solid wall remains on the inside, so that interior space heating is stored in the masonry wall like a storage heater. In addition, in the coming decades of predicted global warming, the property is insulated from excessive solar gains in summertime – besides the fact that adding insulation externally will not result in any loss of floor area internally. However, in many Edwardian properties it is necessary to retain the external appearance of the house, particularly in the case of facing brickwork and other aesthetic finishes, in which case the internal addition of insulation improvements becomes the only viable option, with its inherent technical problems for the unwary. Either way, it is possible to improve the thermal performance of solid walls so that they match the thermal conductivity of current building regulations.[5]

Refurbishment or renovation, such as replacing existing plaster finishes, is an ideal opportunity to install internal insulation. Internal insulation is clearly worthwhile when external insulation is not an option, as most heat is usually lost through the walls of a house because they usually represent the largest surface area for heat loss. However, there are a few disadvantages, such as the loss of floor area, the reduction of thermal mass, and the risk of interstitial condensation. The thermal mass of the solid wall is isolated when internal insulation is installed, which means that the house will heat up and cool down more quickly than with an externally insulated solid wall. The addition of 100mm (4in) of mineral wool fitted between battens will ensure an improved thermal performance close to building regulations, but there are proprietary systems using much thinner rigid insulation to give the same levels of performance. However, care should always be taken to avoid the risk of interstitial condensation, because a traditional construction such as a solid wall needs to breathe. The risk of dampness from condensation is increased when inappropriate vapour checks are added to traditional construction.

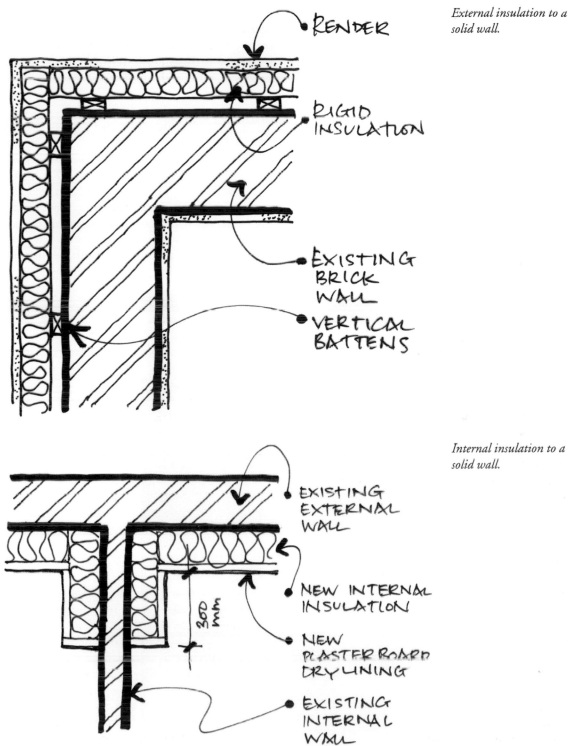

External insulation to a solid wall.

RENDER

RIGID INSULATION

EXISTING BRICK WALL

VERTICAL BATTENS

Internal insulation to a solid wall.

EXISTING EXTERNAL WALL

NEW INTERNAL INSULATION

300 mm

NEW PLASTERBOARD DRY LINING

EXISTING INTERNAL WALL

INTERSTITIAL CONDENSATION

Old houses need to breathe so that the building fabric can dry out the moisture from rainfall, and so the water vapour generated by occupancy can evaporate. The addition of inappropriate vapour checks with high levels of vapour resistance as used in modern construction can create problems in old houses. Water vapour condenses when it meets a cold surface, given the right conditions of humidity and temperature – this is known as the 'dew point temperature'. If this surface is inside the layers of construction, such as a cavity, where conditions are exacerbated by an inappropriate vapour check, this is known as interstitial condensation. To avoid this risk, any vapour check should be placed on the warm side of the internal insulation – that is, the inside. Much of the time a vapour check is not required, or only one of a low vapour resistance, known as a breather membrane. Sometimes a plasterboard internal lining, if well sealed, can suffice with a coat of mineral paint.

CASE STUDIES

Case Study 5.1
Walsall eco-house.

Key Points
- Early Edwardian house, 1903.
- DIY package of measures undertaken over time on a modest budget.
- Loft and hot water cylinder insulation installed first.

Case Study 5.1 Walsall eco-house – front elevation.

- Gas condensing boiler installed, with programmable room thermostat controls.
- Radiator panels with TRVs installed.
- Internal wall insulation undertaken in phases.
- Low energy lighting and appliances installed.
- The energy performance of a modern dwelling achieved in a solid-walled Edwardian house.

General

This early Edwardian house was built in 1903 in Walsall in the West Midlands. Although the back of the house faces south, which is good for passive solar gain, it has solid brick walls. There were some cavity walls in avant garde house designs of this vintage, but this form of construction did not begin to become popular until the 1920s.

The owners who upgraded the property moved into a house that had no insulation and was heated by electric storage heaters in the mid-1980s. They have dramatically improved the energy performance of their house on a modest budget over time so that it now ranks with a modern house in terms of carbon dioxide emissions. They took the obvious measures of installing loft and hot water cylinder insulation as

soon as they moved into the house, but their growing environmental concern inspired them to take more far-reaching measures over time.

Insulation

The insulation of the solid walls was a large and complicated DIY undertaking implemented in prioritized phases, beginning in the 1990s with internal insulation to one bedroom and the bathroom. By the early years of the new century the owners were insulating the party wall between the garage and the house, a task well suited to DIY; this included the addition of 200mm (8in) of external insulation to the wall above the single-storey, lean-to garage – always the best option to minimize cold or thermal bridges. Recycled materials, such as 1960s hardboard doors on battens, were used to enclose the insulation. In 2003 internal wall insulation was added to the dining room, and half of the cost was the expert replacement of the period ceiling coving for £600.[6] Double glazing with a low emissivity coating was also installed at this time, inside the original window in order to preserve it.

The desire for a new kitchen in 2005 provided the impetus to install insulation on the inside of the

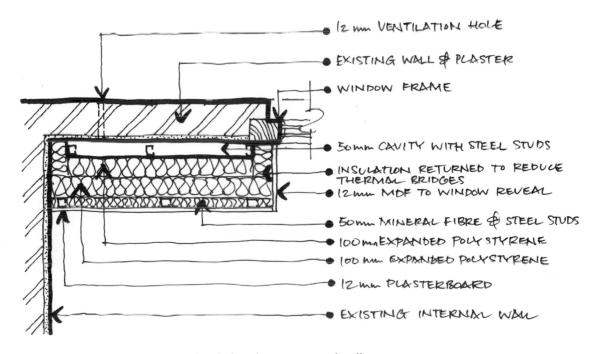

- 12 mm VENTILATION HOLE
- EXISTING WALL & PLASTER
- WINDOW FRAME
- 50mm CAVITY WITH STEEL STUDS
- INSULATION RETURNED TO REDUCE THERMAL BRIDGES
- 12mm MDF TO WINDOW REVEAL
- 50mm MINERAL FIBRE & STEEL STUDS
- 100mm EXPANDED POLYSTYRENE
- 100 mm EXPANDED POLYSTYRENE
- 12mm PLASTERBOARD
- EXISTING INTERNAL WALL

Case Study 5.1 Walsall eco-house – detail of insulation to external wall.

external wall, using 100mm (4in) polyurethane insulation held in place with battens. Cold bridging was reduced by using a 25mm (1in) insulating quilt (sold as sound insulation) over the battens and finishing with plasterboard – the latter layer provides an effective low vapour resistance barrier with carefully filled gaps. Cold bridging to the edge of the solid floor slab in the kitchen was countered by carrying the insulation down 600mm (24in) into a trench backfilled with a weak dry-mix mortar. The remaining two, downstairs, uninsulated walls have bay windows, so they were left until last. One was insulated in 2006/7 using the same technique as in the kitchen – except that 60mm (2½in) polyurethane was used and the battens were omitted. The remaining downstairs room is the subject of a future project.

Heating

By the late nineties the owners had replaced the electric storage heaters with gas central heating from a new condensing combination boiler. Radiators with thermostatic radiator valves (TRVs) were installed by a friendly plumber. A programmable thermostat with room-by-room heating zones was also installed, and all pipe runs were fully insulated. In retrospect the owners would have invested in a more expensive model of the boiler with intelligent room thermostats that would modulate the boiler output down as the desired room temperature is approached. They are also of the opinion that 18–19°C (64–66°F) is a comfortable indoor temperature setting, and prefer to wear a sweater than turn the heating up – they even see it as a benefit in terms of fewer layers of clothing to pull on when they venture outside.

Hot water

Hot water for the shower and the bath is provided by the combination boiler. The small amounts of hot water required in the kitchen and bathroom sinks are provided by individual electric water heaters with 10ltr (2gal) storage capacity – these are not considered an efficient use of the main boiler, and heat would be lost in the longer pipe runs.

Lighting and Appliances

Most lighting is by low energy bulbs (some as low as 5 watts) in either uplighter shades or paper globe shades. Bathroom and bedroom lights are rarely on for any length of time, so 40-watt bulbs are used – the owners last bought a 100-watt bulb twenty years ago! Lighting and appliances began to approach a third of the energy used in the house, with another third for space heating – in line with the energy usage proportions of a modern house. So the owners purchased a plug-in electricity meter to monitor the energy use of individual appliances. The definitive insight that this piece of kit provided led to its nickname 'The Judge'.

Among the horrors that 'The Judge' uncovered was the fact that a halogen desk lamp was using 4 watts of power when switched off! The fridge freezer, which was two decades old, redeemed itself with an external coat of 60mm (2½in) of polyurethane insulation, after they could not find a big enough modern replacement – it is now estimated to have an energy label rating of about 'C'. The dishwasher was using 1.5 KWh each wash, so it was replaced with the Edwardian technique of hand-washing – using about 0.3 KWh of energy for hot water, but with the attendant 'servant problem'. The washing machine is 'A' rated, while the tumble drier was last used in 2004 and sparrows now nest in its ventilation outlet.

Water

A Swedish lavatory was installed, which uses only 2.5 to 4.5ltr (½ to 1gal) of water each flush – this is half the amount of water used by conventional British models.

Top Tips

- Assess your lifestyle
- Take things slowly
- Keep it simple

Energy

The combination of improvements to insulation and the heating system reduced carbon dioxide emissions to just 20 per cent of their original consumption. Electric lighting and appliance improvements reduced consumption by about half.

Case Study 5.2
Semi-detached Edwardian house.

Key Points
- Typical Edwardian, semi-detached house in a conservation area.
- Large kitchen, dining and utility extension constructed to the rear.
- Roof insulation installed to rooms in the roof.
- Gas condensing boiler central heating with TRVs and zoned controls installed.
- Secondary glazing put in.

- Underfloor heating to the rear extension installed.
- Internal insulation to the front elevation is planned.

General
This typically Edwardian semi-detached villa in a conservation area suffered from the usual problem of a small kitchen to the rear, and no garage. The owners decided to incorporate energy efficiency improvements to their extensive additions to the property. The starting point was that the new extension would be energy efficient and in excess of current building

Case Study 5.2 Semi-detached Edwardian house – front elevation.

Case Study 5.2 Semi-detached Edwardian house – low emissivity, double-glazed window.

regulation standards – this was coupled with improvements such as roof space insulation to new rooms in the attic, secondary glazing and a new heating system.

A panel radiator central heating system was installed when the present owners moved into the property, but the thermostatic radiator valves were not installed optimally – they were in a vertical position, which meant that the rising hot air from the distribution pipe below affected the temperature setting. The installation of a new gas condensing boiler heating system with zoned controls allowed for the rectification of this common error, and the optimal positioning of TRVs in a horizontal position. Underfloor heating was installed in the new extension, which allows the condensing boiler to operate at optimal low temperatures, and prevents the stratification of hot air near the high ceilings.

The extension means that much of the original external solid wall is now an internal wall, but there are plans to install insulation on the inside walls of the front elevation.

Case Study 5.2 Semi-detached Edwardian house – secondary glazing.

SUMMARY

- The turn of the nineteenth into the twentieth century heralded many social and technological changes, not least of which were in domestic architecture. Edwardian domestic architecture bridges the gap between late Victorian suburbs and the speculative housing styles of inter-war suburbia.
- The Edwardian semi-detached house became the norm for middle-class housing, largely inspired by the Arts and Crafts Movement. The artistic house lay at the stylistic roots of Edwardian suburban developments, with its emphasis on health, sanitation, fresh air and light.
- The dawn of domestic electric lighting was, however, reaching middle-class suburbs in the Edwardian period, and it allowed a new outlook in terms of interior design. Electric light quickly became a status symbol and the harbinger of a more profligate age in terms of the use of energy in general. We now each use several times the energy that a typical Edwardian did.
- A typical unimproved Edwardian house is using nearly two-thirds of its energy on space heating. The improvement of thermal insulation and space-heating energy efficiency is also typically the most cost-effective way to begin improving the performance of an Edwardian house.
- The only way to improve the thermal conductive properties of a solid wall is to add insulation on the inside or the outside. Usually, the way to improve

Case Study 5.2 Semi-detached Edwardian house – thermostatic radiator valve, incorrect installation.

Case Study 5.2 Semi-detached Edwardian house – thermostatic radiator valve, correct installation.

the insulation of solid walls with the least technical risk is to add insulation to the outside – creating a 'warm wall' that largely avoids cold or
thermal bridging.

- Internal insulation is clearly worthwhile when
external insulation is not an option, as most heat is
usually lost through the walls of a house because
they usually represent the largest surface area for
heat loss.

- The disadvantages of internal insulation as
opposed to external insulation are the loss of floor
area, the reduction of thermal mass, and the risk of
interstitial condensation.

- Old houses need to breathe so that the building
fabric can dry out the moisture from rainfall, and
so the water vapour generated by occupancy can
evaporate. The addition of inappropriate vapour
checks with high levels of vapour resistance as used
in modern construction can create problems in old
houses.

- Case studies show that with the right combination
of improvements and lifestyle, a solid-walled
Edwardian house can be brought up to the energy
efficiency performance of a modern dwelling.

CHAPTER 6

Inter-War: 1918–1939

OVERVIEW

World War I provided the catalyst for mass social housing in Britain. Lloyd George promised 'homes fit for heroes' for returning combatants, after the generally poor health of the working population recruited to fight the war was publicized. The Walters report in 1918 recommended that local authorities should be subsidized to build housing for rent, at lower density than the average in Victorian terraced housing. Raymond Unwin, the architect and planner who was the father of the garden city movement, was influential in the select committee and the subsequent report. Home ownership also expanded, as mortgages were easier to obtain.

Four million homes were built between 1919 and

Typical inter-war houses, London – 'Tudorbethan style'.

Typical inter-war houses, London – 'Tudorbethan style'.

1939, and three million of them were speculatively built. Most of these were the ubiquitous and popular semi-detached, suburban, mock-Tudor house – built to a formula with bay windows at the front and French windows overlooking the still expansive rear garden. Due to the shortage of skilled labour and essential materials, about a quarter of a million dwellings of this new housing stock were constructed by non-traditional methods and materials.[1]

Among the new methods of construction that were developed were more than twenty steel-framed housing systems, along with other systems based on pre-

cast and *in situ* concrete, timber, and occasionally cast iron.[2] Some of these were more successful than others, resulting in varying levels of building performance over the years, and there was usually a switch to traditional techniques whenever the labour and materials supply allowed. The use of non-traditional techniques was, however, more extensive in Scotland, due to widespread supply problems.

Despite some new radical domestic construction techniques, most housing conformed stylistically to mock historical styles – including applied decorative half-timbering, with bays and dormers inspired by the vernacular architectural revival of the turn of the century. The minimal, flat-roofed appearance of Modernism and Art Deco also began to creep into mainstream housing developments, but was far less popular than the stereotypical, suburban 'semi'.

Inter-war private housing developments were usually of a lower density, causing problems of 'ribbon' and 'pepper pot' development, made possible by low petrol prices. Ribbon developments, along arterial roads, exacerbated the perception of housing incursion into rural areas, among other problems. Pepper pot developments, on the other hand, made vehicular access more difficult, as they were isolated houses in rural locations. The sprawling, speculative, suburban housing boom of the 1920s and 1930s invaded the British landscape like the tentacles of an octopus, which inspired the title of an influential book by Clough Williams-Ellis. The architect of Portmeirion created the catalyst for new legislation with his book *England and the octopus*, published in 1928. The provocatively argued book started a polemic that led to the passing of the Prevention of Ribbon Development Act and the London Green Belt Act, shortly afterwards. They were the precursors of the modern planning system.

Typical Art Deco flats, London.

Modernist-inspired detached house, Hatfield, Hertfordshire.

CAVITY WALLS

Cavity walls were occasionally used in buildings since at least the early decades of the nineteenth century, using a narrow cavity with brick or stone ties to hold the leaves of the construction together. They were usually used in prestigious buildings to improve comfort by reducing the passage of moisture to the interior of the building. *Avant garde* architects, such as those leading the Arts and Crafts Movement, often used cavity walls and other innovative technology in their country houses in the latter decades of the nineteenth and early twentieth century.

The cavity wall became increasingly popular for widespread use in domestic architecture in the 1920s and 1930s, but still primarily as a 'rainscreen' to increase comfort and protect the inner leaf of the wall from being soaked by rainwater. The fact that it also promoted improved thermal comfort, with wider cavities at least, was, initially, an added benefit, and it was not until much later that insulation was added to the cavities in cavity-walled construction. The widespread use of insulation in cavity walls began in the 1970s and became part of the building regulations in the 1990s.

A solid wall of brickwork contains both 'header' and 'stretcher' bricks, with the header bricks acting to

Modernist-inspired semi-detached house, Hatfield, Hertfordshire.

The development of the cavity wall.

Date	Development	Cavity width (mm)
1920s	Cavity wall starts to become popular	Variable
1930s	Cavity walls become main form of construction	Variable
1940s	Cavity width becomes standardised	50
1950s	Concrete blocks are used for inner leaf	50
1960s	Lightweight 'aircrete' blocks are introduced	50
1970s	Cavity width is increased	60–70
1980s	Cavity wall insulation starts to be introduced	60–70

Solid wall brick bond – Flemish bond.

Solid wall brick bond – English bond.

Cavity wall brick bond – stretcher bond.

tie the construction together in brick bonds such as English or Flemish bond. Cavity walls contain only stretcher bricks, or bricks placed lengthways, with a similar inner leaf, and both tied together with metal wall ties that span the cavity. So it is easy to tell whether a wall is solid, or is in the then new-fangled cavity construction technique, simply by observing which type of brick bonding you have on your inter-war house – even if the walls are rendered, there will usually be a plinth of brickwork, or some brickwork somewhere, as a tell-tale. Adding insulation to the wall cavity reduces heat loss through walls by up to 40 per cent, and is the single most cost-effective insulation measure after loft insulation.[3]

FLOORS

Most Georgian and Victorian houses, in towns and cities at least, were provided with a basement or cellar storey – but such hard-won and uneconomic space was unfashionable in the inter-war speculative building boom. However, most inter-war houses were built with suspended timber floors, or a combination of solid and timber floors. Solid concrete floors followed a similar evolution to the cavity wall – beginning with an uninsulated solid floor laid on a DPM over hardcore, which conducts heat from the house directly into the ground. Heat is lost through a suspended timber floor via the gaps in the construction and the intentional draughts created by the air bricks which ventilate underneath the floor. The floor timbers would quickly become damp without such ventilation and eventually rot away, but construction gaps in the floor should be improved to reduce draughts inside the house. Floorboards in suspended timber floors were later built with tongue-in-groove joints to reduce such draughts. It is only relatively recently that building regulations have required the addition of insulation to both types of ground floor, to meet improved U-value standards.

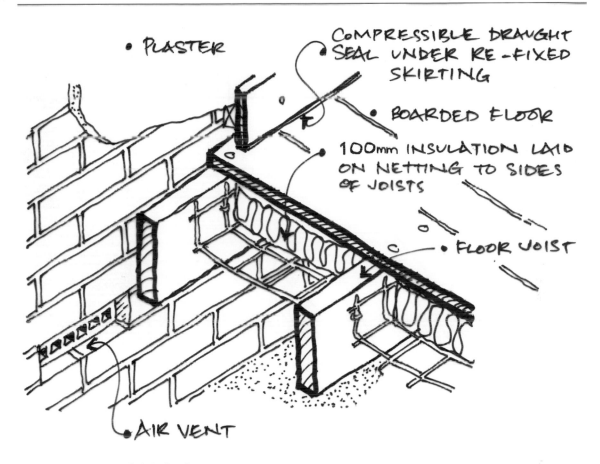

- PLASTER
- COMPRESSIBLE DRAUGHT SEAL UNDER RE-FIXED SKIRTING
- BOARDED FLOOR
- 100mm INSULATION LAID ON NETTING TO SIDES OF JOISTS
- FLOOR JOIST
- AIR VENT

Insulation to a suspended timber floor.

Solid concrete floors were becoming popular in some of the leading housing developments in the late nineteenth century, but most inter-war floors are usually constructed with at least some suspended timber joists and floorboards. Adding insulation to suspended timber floors is easiest if there is access from below, such as from a cellar or crawl space, or if the floorboards are being removed and replaced. This is also a good time to ensure that any water pipes below the floor are well insulated. Adding insulation to a suspended timber floor should also improve air-tightness and reduce draughts, but care should be taken to ensure the continuity of the insulation and necessary ventilation. A flexible sealant should be placed underneath the skirting board when it is replaced to reduce air gaps, but suspended timber floors need ventilation from airbricks – so these should not be blocked up.

Refurbishing or replacing solid concrete ground floors or their screeds also provides an ideal opportunity to add insulation. Solid concrete slabs are the most difficult type of floor to retrofit with insulation. Adding rigid insulation on top of an existing solid floor will obviously raise the level of the new floor finish – so doors will need to be shortened. Some modern insulation materials are still effective, to a lesser extent, in very thin layers, so that increases to the floor levels are minimized. As a general rule, 25mm (1in) of polystyrene or 40mm (1½in) of polyisocyanurate foam will improve the U-value of a solid floor to levels approaching modern building regulation standards. But a little added insulation is better than no insulation at all, and even only 5mm (¼in) of rubber foam is better than nothing, and will reduce heat loss through the floor and improve comfort levels.

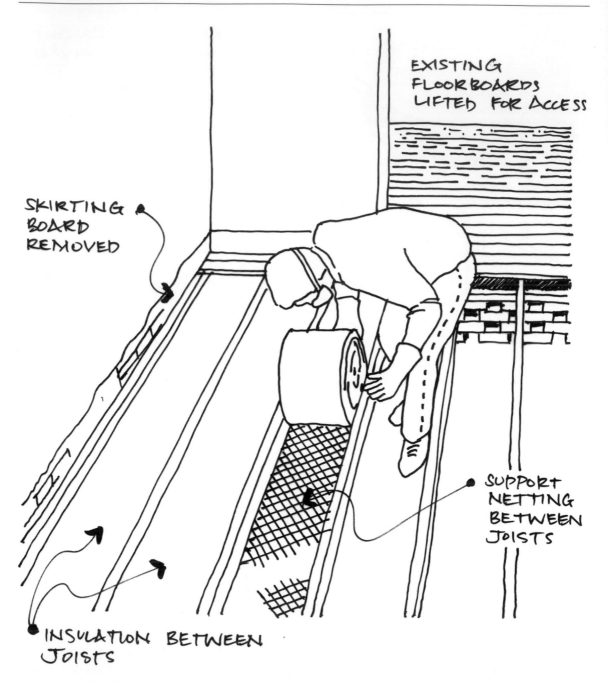

Laying insulation to a suspended timber floor.

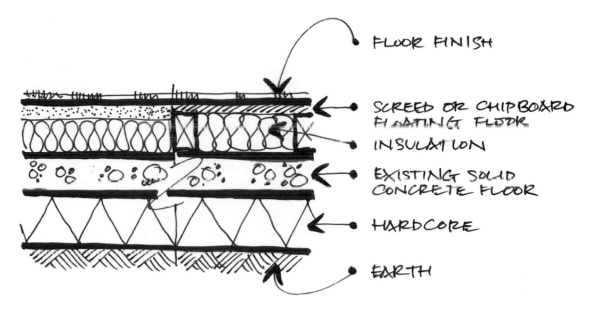

Insulation to solid floors.

FLAT ROOFS

The influence of the Modern Movement and architectural inspiration from continental Europe, where the climate is more conducive to this form of construction, led to the use of flat roofs in the domestic architecture of the inter-war period. Although flat-roofed houses were ultimately less popular than pitched-roof varieties, there are also many houses of this period that have acquired later flat-roofed extensions. Some of the original flat roofs were solid

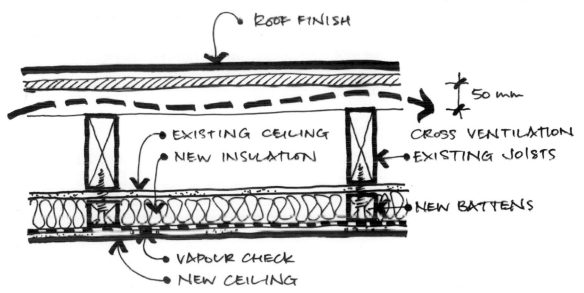

Insulation to flat roofs – cold deck.

reinforced concrete, the preferred construction material of Modern Movement architects. But the majority are likely to be constructed from timber, and if any insulation were subsequently added, it is invariably to the inside of the structural timber. This is known as a 'cold roof', because the structure is on the cold side of the insulation – that is, nearer to the outside.

The ventilation of cold roofs is essential, as the cold surface of the structure could cause condensation or interstitial condensation. It is possible to upgrade an uninsulated timber flat roof by placing insulation between the joists that support the deck and waterproof membrane, but such 'cold roofs' are no longer recommended due to the difficulty of ensuring effective ventilation of the void – a 'warm roof' is preferred.

A warm deck flat roof has insulation above the deck and joists, covered by a waterproof membrane – the structure elements are on the warm side of the construction, closest to the heated interior. A variation of the warm roof is called an 'inverted warm roof' – this is where rigid insulation is placed above the waterproof membrane and weighed down by stone chippings or paving slabs. If the waterproof membrane of the flat roof has reached the end of its life and is being replaced, a warm roof upgrade should be considered. This also provides an opportunity to improve the drainage of a flat roof, by introducing tapered insulation, which should reduce the 'ponding' of rainwater. Rainwater which collects and lies in ponds on flat roofs due to inadequate falls to drainage outlets is a common problem – it increases the structural loading and reduces the life of the waterproof membrane, quite apart from looking unsightly and providing a potential breeding ground for aquatic insect life.

An inverted warm roof solution is generally less preferable than a warm roof where the increased thickness of the subsequent roof construction is not problematic. And as the inverted warm roof entails the addition of ballast material, the roof structure should be checked to ensure that it can take the additional weight – this is rarely the case with timber flat roof structures. It is also possible to create warm

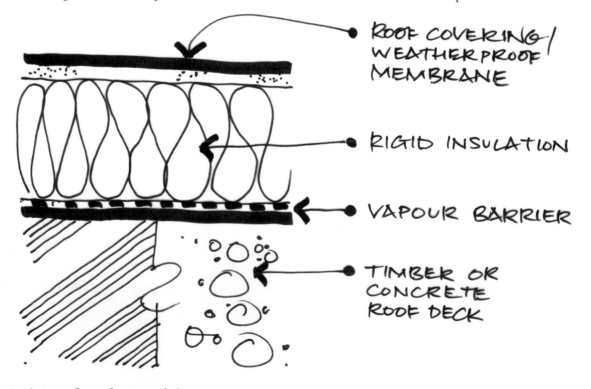

Insulation to flat roofs – warm deck.

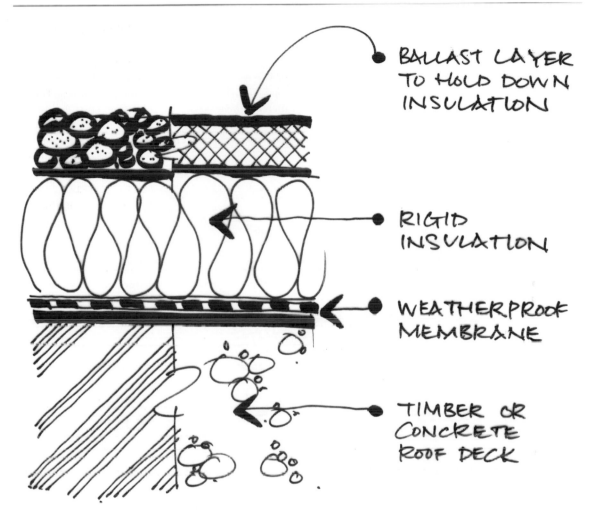

BALLAST LAYER TO HOLD DOWN INSULATION

RIGID INSULATION

WEATHERPROOF MEMBRANE

TIMBER OR CONCRETE ROOF DECK

Insulation to flat roofs – inverted warm deck.

roof constructions by applying a new waterproof membrane over the top of the existing waterproof membrane of an uninsulated roof. If it is not practical to increase the thickness of the roof with a warm roof approach, internal insulation should be applied to the ceiling. Insulation-backed plasterboard is applied in a similar way to internal wall insulation, but to the ceiling, which has less risk of condensation than a cold roof construction.

Similar principles, in terms of warm, cold and inverted roofs, apply to solid concrete flat roofs. The generally preferred way of insulating a solid flat roof is to add rigid insulation above the roof deck – making

it a warm roof if the insulation is below the weatherproof membrane. The roof becomes an inverted warm roof if the insulation is placed above the weatherproofing membrane, in which case a layer of ballast is placed on top to hold the insulation in place. Clearly, the retrofitted roof must be capable of withstanding the additional weight placed on it, particularly if a ballast layer is added, which could be quite heavy in the case of materials such as concrete paving slabs. This also provides opportunities, where the structure allows, to create roof terraces on top of retrofitted solid flat roofs.

THERMAL BRIDGES

Most inter-war houses were constructed with little thought of thermal or cold bridges, as they were usually solid-walled, or uninsulated cavity walls. There was usually no consideration of the position of insulation in the construction layers, because there was usually no insulation when they were originally constructed! Heat will follow the easiest path from the heated interior space to the cold outdoors – the path with the least resistance. Solid elements, such as window cills or lintels over windows made of materials such as concrete or stone, which connect the warm inside and the cold exterior, make ideal cold or thermal bridges in the house's construction envelope. Clearly, such thermal bridges will significantly increase heat losses and heating costs in an old house, and because they have a lower surface temperature than the surrounding construction, they will increase risks of internal condensation, damp and discomfort.

Typical thermal or cold bridge – window reveal.

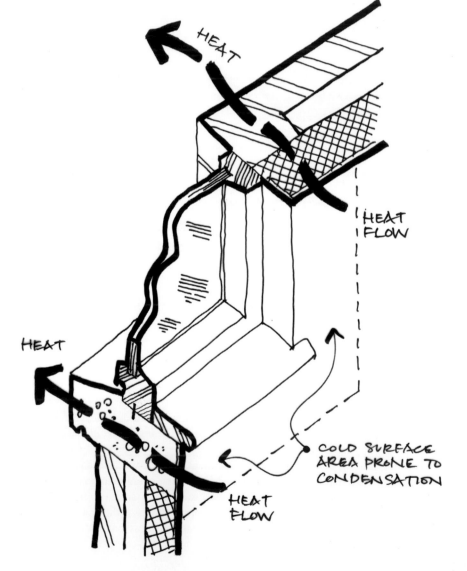

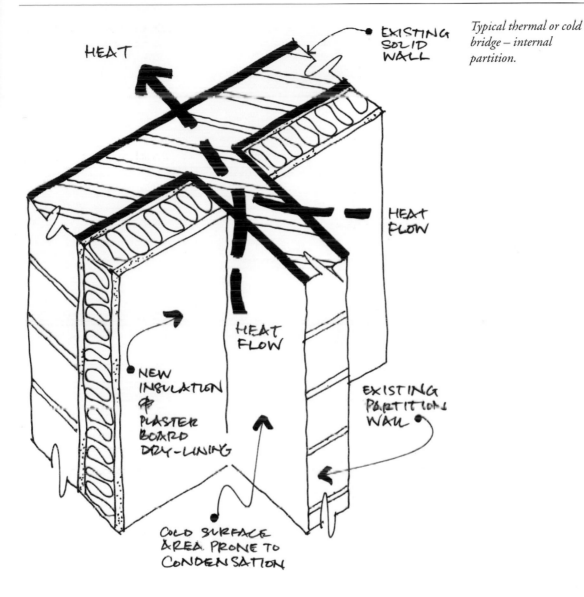

HEAT

EXISTING
SOLID
WALL

Typical thermal or cold bridge – internal partition.

HEAT
FLOW

NEW
INSULATION
&
PLASTER
BOARD
DRY-LINING

HEAT
FLOW

EXISTING
PARTITIONS
WALL

COLD SURFACE
AREA PRONE TO
CONDENSATION

The only way to virtually eliminate thermal bridges when adding insulation to old houses is to adopt a 'warm overcoat' principle – to wrap the house in a continuous and contiguous layer of insulation. This would necessitate the use of external insulation to the walls and floors, as well as a warm roof insulation upgrade. Such radical interventions are not always convenient, and are obviously only contemplated when a major refurbishment is under way, such as replacing old floors and roof coverings. They may also not be technically possible or aesthet-

ically desirable. However, there are ways to minimize thermal bridging when adding layers of insulation internally, by considering the typical construction details of the house and ensuring careful attention to detail. After all, it would be a shame to partially undo all the good work done by insulating the house, by allowing thermal bridges to occur – and there is always the risk that you might introduce new problems, such as condensation, by not minimizing thermal bridges.[4]

109

Re-roofing an inter-wars house and adding insulation above the rafters (warm roof).

CASE STUDIES

Case Study 6.1

Typical inter-war house.

Key Points
- Loft insulation top-up to 250mm (10in) of mineral wool insulation.
- Dry-lining with insulated plasterboard to solid brick walls.
- SEDBUK 'A'-rated gas condensing boiler.
- Room thermostat, programmer and TRVs.
- Humidity-controlled extractor to kitchen and bathroom.
- Energy-efficient light bulbs and 'A'-rated white goods.
- Timber-framed double-glazing with low emissivity glass and trickle vents.
- Draught lobby porch and insulated external doors.
- Draught excluders to doors, windows, loft hatch and skirting boards, and controlled ventilation to fireplaces and chimneys.
- 100mm mineral wool insulation to timber suspended floors.
- SAP rating of 45 per cent improved to 75 per cent, which is above post-1990 average SAP ratings of 65 per cent.
- Energy costs reduced by 75 per cent.

SUMMARY

- World War I provided the catalyst for mass social housing in Britain. Home ownership also expanded, as mortgages were easier to obtain. Four million homes were built between 1919 and 1939, and three million of them were speculatively built. Shortages of skilled labour and essential materials meant that about a quarter of a million dwellings

Case Study 6.1 Typical inter-war semi-detached house.

were constructed with non-traditional methods and materials.

- Despite some new radical domestic construction techniques, most housing conformed stylistically to mock historical styles – including applied decorative half-timbering, with bays and dormers inspired by the vernacular architectural revival of the turn of the century. The minimal, flat-roofed appearance of Modernism and Art Deco also began to creep into mainstream housing developments, but was far less popular than the stereotypical, suburban 'semi'.
- Inter-war private housing developments were usually of a lower density, causing problems of 'ribbon' and 'pepper pot' development, made possible by low petrol prices. The sprawling, speculative, suburban housing boom of the 1920s led to the passing of the Prevention of Ribbon Development Act and the London Green Belt Act. These were the precursors of the modern planning system.

- The cavity wall became increasingly popular for widespread use in domestic architecture in the 1920s and 1930s, but still primarily as a 'rain-screen' to increase comfort and protect the inner leaf of the wall from being soaked by rainwater. It was not until much later that insulation was added to the cavities. The widespread use of insulation in cavity walls began in the 1970s and became part of the building regulations in the 1990s.
- A solid wall of brickwork contains both 'header' and 'stretcher' bricks, with the header bricks acting to tie the construction together in brick bonds such as English or Flemish bond. Cavity walls contain only stretcher bricks, or bricks placed lengthways, known as stretcher bond – so it is easy to tell whether a wall is solid or cavity-wall construction. Adding insulation to cavity walls reduces heat loss through walls by up to 40 per cent, and is the single most cost-effective insulation measure after loft insulation.

- Most inter-war houses were built with suspended timber floors, or a combination of solid and timber floors. Heat is lost through a suspended timber floor via the gaps in the construction and the intentional draughts created by the air bricks that ventilate underneath the floor. It is only relatively recently that building regulations have required the addition of insulation to both types of ground floor, to meet improved U-value standards.
- Adding insulation to suspended timber floors is easiest if there is access from below, such as from a cellar, or if the floorboards are being removed and replaced. Refurbishing or replacing solid concrete ground floors or their screeds also provides an ideal opportunity to add insulation. Solid concrete slabs are the most difficult type of floor to retrofit with insulation.

- Flat roofs are constructed and thermally improved in three main ways: cold roof, warm roof, and inverted warm roof. The timber structure of cold roofs has to be ventilated, but 'cold roofs' are no longer recommended due to the difficulty of ensuring effective ventilation of the void – a 'warm roof' is preferred.
- Heat flows along the easiest path from the heated interior space to the cold outdoors. Consequently solid elements, such as window sills or lintels over windows made of materials such as concrete or stone, which connect the warm inside and the cold exterior, make ideal cold or thermal bridges in the house's construction envelope. There are ways to minimize thermal bridging with careful attention to detail when upgrading your inter-war house.

CHAPTER 7

Post-War: 1945–1980

OVERVIEW

The aftermath of World War II created an even greater need for mass housing development than the Great War, not to mention the need to rebuild housing damaged by enemy aircraft. The Ministry of Health predicted future housing demand in early 1943, and a strategy to cope with estimated post-war demand was devised at the beginning of 1944. The Reconstruction Committee's proposal involved a three-staged timetable, starting with an emergency period for the first few years to try and house all those who needed accommodation; the following five years concentrated on new housing construction; and the final period of ten years was aimed at replacing sub-standard and slum housing.

It was hoped that nearly half-a-million permanent dwellings would be provided in the initial emergency period of two years – including around 200,000 dwellings with a short and finite design life. The Burt and Dudley committees were convened in 1942 to consider non-traditional construction techniques to overcome labour and skills shortages, and planning and space standards to reflect lifestyle changes, respectively. Social surveys revealed that a small detached house or bungalow was preferred over a flat by the vast majority of the population – the semi-detached house in a suburb continued as a compromise of this aspiration.

The only possible answer to the sheer scale and scope of post-war housing demand was seen as prefabrication. The problems were different from those faced after World War I, in that material shortages were less crucial than the supply of skilled labour. In addition, the surplus of steel and aluminium produc-tion caused by the war effort dictated housing experimentation with materials such as these. The most ubiquitous type of steel-framed house was the British Iron and Steel Federation (BISF) house designed by Frederick Gibberd, while the Airey and the Wate's house were typical of the concrete systems. The aircraft industry contributed lightweight, aluminium-framed and clad systems, such as the AIROH (Aircraft Industries' Research Organisation on Housing) bungalow and the ARCON house[1] (ARCON stands for 'architectural consultants', and was a practice of architects who worked closely with companies such as ICI and Turners Asbestos Cement Co. Ltd).

The decades following World War II saw the philosophy of house construction changing towards that of industrialized building, with as much work as possible transferred from the site to the factory. However, public confidence waned after the Ronan Point collapse, which involved large panel, off-site construction. High-rise housing buildings were already controversial for social reasons, but Ronan Point raised technical doubts as well. Ronan Point was a twenty-two storey point-block with an inherently strong structure, but it was not designed to withstand the large gas explosion that caused its partial collapse. The explosion occurred in a corner flat on the eighteenth floor and caused the floors above to lift, as they were unrestrained without vertical loading – the panels were blown outwards, and this led to the progressive collapse of the whole building. Other construction problems were found in some of the other large panel buildings.

Volumetric systems, using a series of prefabricated 'boxes' that were connected on site, were also used

Typical post-war detached houses, London.

Typical post-war semi-detached houses, St Albans, Hertfordshire.

Typical 1960s block of flats, London.

Typical 1960s block of flats, London.

during the sixties and seventies. For obvious reasons, these usually involved lightweight timber or metal frames – following on from earlier volumetric aluminium bungalows from the immediate post-war period.

The 1950s and 1960s also saw the continuation of traditional building techniques, and the gradual improvement of the thermal efficiency of building fabric to at least improving building regulation standards. The energy crises of the early and mid-seventies gave further impetus to legislative and house owners' energy efficiency improvements. In this respect, the adage that 'history repeats itself' is appropriate in the first decade of the twenty-first century, with the added incentives of global warming and climate change.

ENERGY EFFICIENCY

The Energy Saving Trust estimates that a typical post-war house, built in around 1970, is emitting 5 tonnes of carbon dioxide every year – compared to 4 tonnes from a new-build house from the mid-1990s, and probably about 3 tonnes from a new house built to present building regulation standards. The typical post-war house has cavity walls, some loft insulation (25mm/1in), double glazing, and is normally centrally heated by a gas boiler. Typically, this also means that a post-war house is using nearly half of its energy on space heating, with water heating and lights and appliances making up the other half. The improvement of thermal insulation and space-heating energy efficiency is also typically the most cost-effective way to begin improving the performance of a post-war house.

Although modest energy efficiency improvements were usually made, over the decades, to post-war houses – such as 50–100mm (2–4in) loft insulation, new boiler and radiators, double glazing, draught-proofing and some low energy lighting – these will not bring the house up to current standards, and more appropriate improvements are required to do this, such as:

- add more loft insulation, up to 250–300mm (10–12in);
- add cavity wall insulation;
- add a new condensing boiler;
- improve the heating and hot water controls;
- add a well insulated hot water cylinder;
- install low energy lighting;
- choose appliances that are energy efficient.[2]

Stretcher-bond brickwork to a cavity wall.

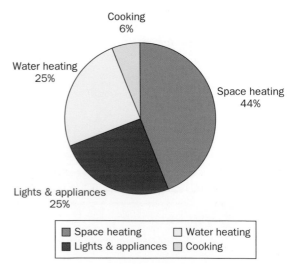

Typical energy use in a post-war house.

Cavity Wall Insulation

Cavity wall domestic construction became standard in post-war houses, with a 50mm (2in) air cavity – but it wasn't until the early 1980s that thermal efficiency standards in the building regulations normally required the addition of insulation to the wall cavity. About 30 per cent of the space heating lost from an uninsulated post-war house is through the walls, and installing retrofitted cavity wall insulation reduces heat loss through walls by up to 60 per cent. Insulating cavity walls in a post-war house could save up to 25 per cent of heating costs with a payback period of a few years.

Cavity fill is the most cost-effective insulation energy-efficiency upgrade after loft insulation. Most existing cavity walls are suitable for insulation improvements – but suitability depends on the local site exposure to weather such as driving rain, the condition of the existing construction, and the choice of particular insulation materials. Dwellings that are, in general, more exposed to prevailing winds and driving rain will usually be on the western shores of the British Isles, but conditions will also depend on localized micro-climates, such as local sheltering from other buildings and trees, or increased exposure on the edge of escarpments. An assessment of each house's suitability for cavity wall insulation fill should be undertaken in all cases.[3]

The installation of cavity wall insulation requires the services of a specialist contractor, who should provide a CIGA (Cavity Insulation Guarantee Agency) guarantee, which normally insures the installation for twenty-five years. Installation is usually straightforward in suitable walls of less than 12m (40ft) in height, and some products are certified in walls of heights up to 25m (80ft). The choice of insulation materials to fill the cavity ranges from mineral wool and polystyrene beads to various foam products – these will vary to some extent in their thermal effectiveness and environmental impact. However, mineral wool, polystyrene beads and many of the foam products have similar levels of thermal resistance and environmental impact, including the embodied energy in their manufacture. Clearly, the main proviso for insulation products suitable for retrofitting cavity walls is that they are capable of being retrospectively blown into the existing cavity, which unfortunately dictates against the use of many natural materials.

An assessment inspection of the cavity wall to confirm its suitability for insulation fill is essential, and cavities of less than 50mm (2in) width are not normally filled. Any general building problems, such as dampness or defects in the wall mortar, should be rectified before installation of cavity fill insulation. Installation normally takes about a day and involves:

- drilling a series of insulation injection holes in the mortar joints of the wall at spacings of around 1m (40in);
- installing cavity barriers, such as at the top of the wall (the eaves), so that there is no overflow of insulation;
- sleeving air ventilators that cross the cavity, or sealing them if they are no longer in use – ventilation grilles to suspended timber floors must be maintained;
- pumping or blowing the insulation material into the cavity;
- quality assurance checks to the installation to ensure there are no gaps;
- making good the injection holes, and ensuring that the cavity is sealed.

Air Infiltration

Unwanted air leakage or infiltration is one of the primary causes of heat loss and discomfort in post-war houses. The term 'infiltration' is used to describe unwanted and unnecessary draughts, as opposed to controlled ventilation required for comfort and safety. Post-war houses, due to the modern impervious nature of their construction, do not generally require the same levels of ventilation that traditionally built houses do to conserve their fabric from damp, so the air-tightness of the post-war dwelling is something to pursue with some vigour, to make them more energy efficient and comfortable. There are many common air leakage paths in post-war houses.

However, as we spend an increasing amount of time indoors, up to 90 per cent of our time in some cases, it is important to maintain healthy and adequate levels of controlled ventilation, or air changes, in our dwellings. Such controlled background ventilation is maintained by the use of devices such as trickle vents in windows, the introduction of passive vents where appropriate, and extractor fans in bathrooms and

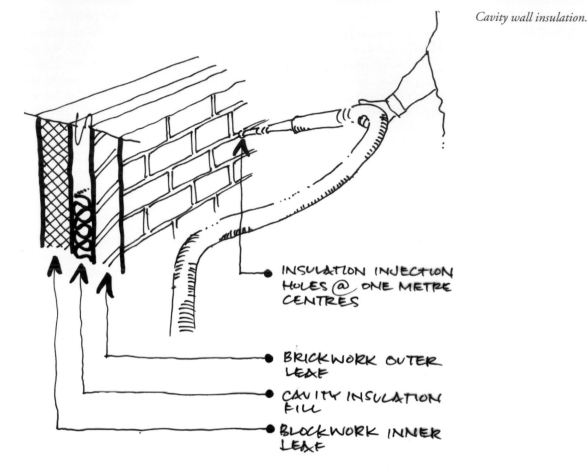

Cavity wall insulation.

INSULATION INJECTION HOLES @ ONE METRE CENTRES

BRICKWORK OUTER LEAF

CAVITY INSULATION FILL

BLOCKWORK INNER LEAF

kitchens. The fact that many modern, synthetic, chemically based products – such as carpets, furnishings, cleaning products and many modern building products – release a wide variety of airborne toxins, reinforces the need for adequate levels of natural ventilation to avoid 'sick building' syndrome – or the 'sick house'. The alternative is to pursue the idea of the natural house, which may be possible from the starting point of some old houses.

The production of synthetic chemicals took off at an exponential rate from the beginning of the twentieth century, and doubled between 1965 and the mid-seventies. Presumably the oil crisis of that decade slowed development. Increased environmental awareness and the rediscovery of natural alternatives in recent decades have also reduced reliance on synthetic products.[4] Types of indoor air pollution in the home include:

- moisture from the kitchen and bathroom;
- carbon monoxide (CO) from boilers and smoking;
- VOCs (volatile organic compounds) from aerosols and synthetic materials in some furnishings and building products – for example formaldehyde – which can give off gas from carpets and furniture;
- allergens from house-dust mites;
- carbon dioxide (CO_2) from the inhabitants and boilers;
- odours from cooking, people and pets.[5]

Draughtproofing

Draughtproofing is one of the most cost-effective energy efficiency improvements to undertake in a post-war house, usually with a payback period of a few years. The average British house has a total area of around 0.18sq m (2sq ft) of air leaks when all the gaps

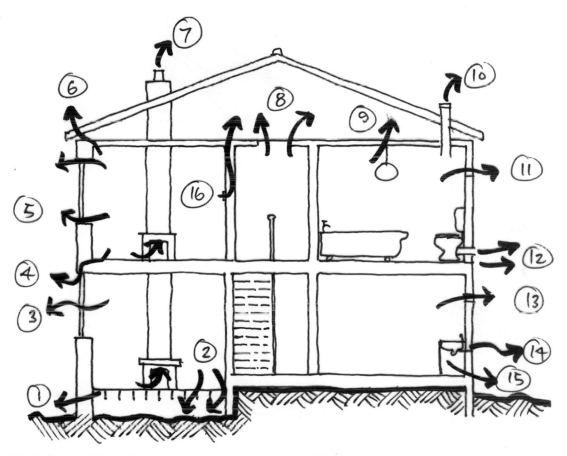

1 Underfloor ventilator grilles
2 Gaps in and around suspended timber floors
3 Leaky windows or doors
4 Pathways through floor/ceiling voids into cavity walls
  and then to the outside
5 Gaps around windows
6 Gaps at the ceiling to wall joint at the eaves
7 Open chimneys
8 Gaps around loft hatches

9 Service penetrations through ceilings
10 Vents penetrating the ceiling/roof
11 Bathroom wall vent or extract fans
12 Gaps around bathroom waste pipes
13 Kitchen wall vent or extractor fan
14 Gaps around kitchen waste pipes
15 Gaps around floor to wall joints
16 Gaps in and around electrical fittings with conduits

Typical air-leakage paths in a post-war house.

are added together. Doors, windows and loft hatches are the obvious places to start, but there are other opportunities:

- Unwanted gaps and cracks in the building fabric should be sealed.
- Letter boxes are often overlooked – a letter box cover reduces draughts.
- Curtains, blinds and shutters are often effective draught excluders.

- Sealing loft hatches prevents heat loss, but also prevents warm moist air from rotting timbers in the roof space.
- Covering timber floorboards with a thick underlay reduces draughts.

Condensing Boilers

Condensing boilers are highly efficient boilers that were introduced to the UK in the 1980s, and since

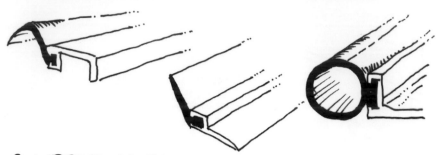

Typical draughtstripping.

COMPRESSION SEALS

GOOD FOR EXTERNAL DOORS – AS THEY ALLOW FOR SEASONAL MOVEMENT OF THE DOOR

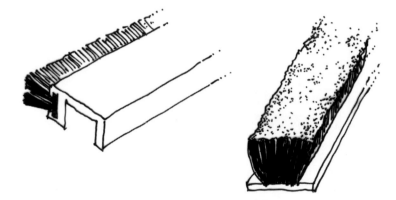

LOW FRICTION OR WIPER SEALS

SUITABLE FOR MOST DOOR & WINDOW TYPES.
GOOD FOR SLIDING DOORS & WINDOWS
RUBBER BLADE WIPER SEALS ARE GOOD FOR
WOODEN DOORS & CASEMENT WINDOWS.

then the technology has improved further. They have efficiencies of around 90 per cent, compared to older boilers of 55–65 per cent efficiency. Some erroneous misconceptions about condensing boilers still abound, such as:

- they have to fully condense to be efficient;
- they are expensive;
- they need larger radiators;
- they are less reliable;
- they are difficult to install;
- they are harder to maintain;
- they cannot be fitted to existing systems;
- they have limited availability;
- the plume of water vapour is a nuisance;
- the condensate is a problem.[6]

CASE STUDIES

Case Study 7.1
Typical post-war house.

Case Study 7.1 Typical post-war semi-detached house.

Key Points

- Loft insulation topped up to 250mm, with mineral wool insulation.
- Cavity fill insulation installed in cavity walls.
- SEDBUK 'A'-rated gas condensing boiler put in.
- Room thermostat, programmer and TRVs installed.
- Humidity-controlled extractor fitted in kitchen and bathroom.
- Energy-efficient light bulbs and 'A'-rated white goods fitted.
- Timber-framed double glazing with low emissivity glass and trickle vents installed.
- Draught lobby porch and insulated external doors constructed.
- Draught excluders added to doors, windows, loft hatch and skirting boards, and controlled ventilation added to fireplaces and chimneys.
- 25mm (1in) rigid insulation added to solid concrete floors.
- SAP rating of 50 per cent improved to 80 per cent, which is above post-1990 average SAP ratings of 65 per cent.
- Energy costs reduced by 50 per cent.

Postscript

The definition of old, particularly within the built environment, is contentious and the subject of much debate. Some maintain that a building has to be one hundred years old to be classified as 'old', and should have achieved a century of longevity before it is considered for listing as part of our architectural heritage. But buildings as young as ten years old are sometimes listed. This book on the energy efficiency of old houses ends in the 1980s, as old houses built before this decade probably present more opportunities and potential for energy efficiency improvements. It is also a convenient place to stop, because the oil and energy crises of the 1970s began to encourage energy conservation in the built environment. Governments began legislation to improve the energy efficiency of new homes, and home owners sought to reduce their spiralling energy bills. But we face new challenges now, of global warming and climate change, not to mention record levels for the price of a barrel of crude oil. This is best summarized in some recent evidence submitted by a past president of the RIBA, to a government report on the existing housing stock in the context of climate change:

If you look back over the last, say, thirty years, the transformation that has already gone on in the housing stock, from coke boilers to natural gas boilers, the amount of double glazing that has gone on, how everybody has insulated their loft, vast change has happened in recent memory, so to say that by 2050 we cannot make substantial changes is unimaginable.[7]

Jack Pringle, Past President of the Royal Institute of British Architects, 2008

The report concludes that:

Reducing carbon emissions by 60 per cent over the next forty-two years requires remarkable change in our habits, our fuel consumption and the technologies we use to build and run our homes. Yet even the most superficial glance back forty-two years is enough to remind us that interplanetary space travel, mobile telephones, the internet, and even heart transplants were then yet to be achieved. The question underlying this report is whether the government can encourage millions of individuals and families, be they in rented flats or homes of their own, to rise to the challenge; but it is, indeed, unimaginable to say that we cannot make substantial change.[8]

SUMMARY

- The aftermath of World War II created an even greater need for mass housing development than the Great War. Social surveys revealed that a small, detached house or bungalow was preferred over a flat by the vast majority of the population – the semi-detached house in a suburb continued as a compromise of this aspiration.
- The decades following World War II saw the philosophy of house construction changing towards that of industrialized building. High-rise housing buildings were already controversial for social reasons, but the Ronan Point disaster raised technical doubts as well.
- The 1950s and 1960s also saw the continuation of traditional building techniques and the gradual improvement of the thermal efficiency of building fabric to at least improving building regulation standards. The energy crises of the early and mid-seventies gave further impetus to legislative and house owners' energy efficiency improvements. In this respect, the adage that history repeats itself is appropriate in the first decade of the twenty-first century, with the added incentives of global warming and climate change.
- The Energy Saving Trust estimates that a typical post-war house, built in around 1970, is emitting 5 tonnes of carbon dioxide every year – compared to 4 tonnes from a new-built house from the mid-1990s, and probably about 3 tonnes from a new house built to present building regulation standards.
- Cavity wall domestic construction became standard in post-war houses. About 30 per cent of the space heating lost from an uninsulated post-war house is through the walls, and installing retrofitted cavity wall insulation reduces heat loss through walls by up to 60 per cent.
- Cavity fill is the most cost-effective insulation energy-efficiency upgrade after loft insulation. Most existing cavity walls are suitable for insulation improvements. An assessment of each house's suitability for cavity wall insulation fill should be undertaken in all cases.
- Unwanted air leakage or infiltration is one of the primary causes of heat loss and discomfort in post-war houses, as opposed to controlled ventilation required for comfort and safety. Air-tightness of the post-war dwelling is something to pursue with some vigour, to make them more energy efficient and comfortable. There are many common air-leakage paths in a post-war house.
- We spend an increasing amount of time indoors, so it is important to maintain healthy and adequate levels of controlled ventilation in our dwellings, as many modern materials release a wide variety of airborne toxins.
- Draughtproofing is one of the most cost-effective energy efficiency improvements to undertake in a post-war house, usually with a payback period of a few years.
- Condensing boilers are highly efficient boilers that were introduced to the UK in the 1980s. They have efficiencies of around 90 per cent, as compared to older boilers of 55–65 per cent efficiency.

CHAPTER 8

Listed Houses and Conservation Areas

INTRODUCTION

About 5 per cent of the housing stock in the UK is 'listed' or in designated conservation areas. This represents about 1¼ million dwellings and about a quarter of all the buildings built before 1919. England has more than 370,000 listed buildings, invariably not constructed to energy efficiency standards that would satisfy present building regulations, but equally invariably the cream of the nation's architectural heritage. England's nearly 10,000 conservation areas contain a further one million unlisted but protected buildings. Buildings that are listed as of special architectural or historic interest, and those in conservation areas, do not have to comply with the energy efficiency standards contained in Part L of the Building Regulations, where compliance would unacceptably alter their character or appearance.

Such houses are viewed as sacrosanct and are not included in any plans for demolition. It is important

Blickling Hall, Norfolk, 1619.

Church End Almshouses, Sarratt, Hertfordshire, 1821.

Semi-detached houses in a conservation area, Sutton Court, North Wembley.

Timber window frames in a conservation area,
Sutton Court, North Wembley.

to find out the status of any house in terms of protective legislation from the local planning office, before making too many plans for upgrading the building fabric, or starting any work on the house. Listed houses are listed because they are important parts of the nation's built heritage, and it is useful to obtain a copy of the information in the listing notes to determine the extent of protection. Advice from professionals who specialize in historic buildings is invaluable when dealing with listed buildings, and their appointment is invariably the first consideration for owners of listed houses. Listed houses are not necessarily large prestigious properties, but are often modest dwellings, such as Georgian almshouses (listed Grade II*) or post-war semi-detached houses in conservation areas.

The extent of fines for interventions to historic buildings taken without 'listed building consent' has gradually increased in value. It is a criminal offence to carry out, or to cause unauthorized works to, a listed building. The Listed Buildings Act 1990 has provisions for fines up to £20,000 and six months imprisonment. As English law is generally based on legal case precedents, and in view of some of the recent court decisions, it is likely that the extent of such fines will increase. Case law currently records fines of up to £75,000. This acts as a good deterrent, and ignorance of the law is no excuse – all of which provides a good case for the relatively economic employment of appropriate construction and property professionals in the area of listed buildings. They will also be liable for any potential breaches of legislation and should carry suitable professional indemnity insurance.

The refurbishment of listed houses and houses in conservation areas is usually limited to measures that do not alter the appearance of the exterior of the house, and sometimes the interiors are also listed. However, there are still many available measures to improve the energy efficiency and environmental sustainability of listed houses, such as increasing levels of insulation, secondary glazing to windows, and upgrading boilers, controls and lighting – without damaging legally protected historic fabric. Aside from the cultural desire to preserve important parts of our built heritage for their historic value, historic messages and attractiveness, there are many other pragmatic reasons for conserving historic houses. Even unprotected houses such as terraced streets have value in terms of context and streetscape, which should not be underestimated.

A strong economic argument for conservation is tourism: an attractive historic environment that attracts tourists depends not only on the few 'great sights', but also on scenic variety – a sense that a place is different and, above all, old. Tourists see qualities in British domestic architecture that many local residents are blasé about. No one can have shown Americans, or other visitors from the New World, around cities such as London, Brighton or Bristol, and not experienced the gasps of horror when they see the depredation wrought by ill-sited high buildings and demolished streets. Seemingly humble examples of British domestic architecture would be given listed status if they were located in the New World.[1]

THE CONSERVATION OF OLD HOUSES

Conservation is the action taken to prevent or slow down decay. In the case of historic buildings, the object is to conserve the continuity of cultural and historic messages contained in the fabric and fittings. Heeding the adage that 'history repeats itself', we have much to learn from the past – and our built environment embodies the most permanent record of our ancestors from which to learn. Minimal intervention on a reversible basis is invariably the best approach: such a philosophy does not prejudice possible future interventions, while avoiding fanciful reconstruction or 'restoration' on the basis of scant evidence. The French archaeologist A. N. Didron stated in 1839 that: 'It is better to preserve than repair, better to repair than restore, better to restore than reconstruct.' Conservation introduces the dimension of time into architectural design.

The foundations of historic building conservation are now enshrined in legislation, listing, scheduling, surveying, town planning, and conservation actions. But it was not always so, as it was only in 1944 that the Town and Country Planning Act took steps towards preservation on a scale more systematic and comprehensive than any country has proposed at any time. This Act was in many ways a response to the ribbon development of suburban houses, sprawling into the countryside. Greenbelts were also established around towns and cities to avoid the development of continuous conurbations across the land. The pepperpot development of isolated rural houses was also targeted.

Sir John Summerson observes possibly the earliest plea for the preservation of ruins on solely cultural grounds, in the Italian architect Leone Battista Alberti's advice (c. 1450) that Roman ruins should be preserved on the site of a new town.[2] Buildings were usually preserved for political or religious reasons in ancient times – reasons of kudos to preserve the established power bases of monarch and church. Alberti's recommendations reflect similar motives to those that finally prompted Great Britain's Ancient Monuments Act of 1912. The Act was a progression from earlier pleas, such as those of the architect of Blenheim Palace, Sir John Vanburgh, for the preservation of Woodstock Manor in 1709, using the argument that buildings are the most valued artefacts of antiquity.

William Morris founded the Society for the Protection of Ancient Buildings (SPAB) in 1877. Morris was inspired by John Ruskin, and outraged at the cavalier fashion in which many ancient buildings were undergoing Victorian 'restorations'. Ruskin felt that the restoration of historic buildings was as bad as, if not worse than demolition, as it often heralded a fanciful and inaccurate replacement of historic building fabric. SPAB was popularly known as 'anti scrape', as it opposed the prevailing Victorian fashion for scraping the continuously applied plaster and limewash off ancient buildings, particularly churches, to expose the stonework. Historically, lime plaster and lime washes were regularly applied to ancient stonework, and other materials, to act as a sacrificial weathering coat for protection against the elements. SPAB felt that such actions were destructive as they destroyed the patina of age and left the stonework vulnerable to decay, solely in the name of a prevailing vogue for the 'picturesque'. Morris concurred with Ruskin's philosophy of conserving historic monuments to retain the patina of their ageing process and evidence of their history. However, it wasn't until 1882 that the Ancient Monument Protection Act was passed, which gave the first statutory protection to a handful of fifty ancient monuments in England, Scotland and Wales.[3]

ADAPTIVE USE

The recent conservation revolution of the 1970s and 1980s has rekindled preservation on cultural grounds. Although arguably with less to conserve, the phenomenon is no less intense in America. Vincent Scully, possibly America's foremost architectural teacher and historian, calls it 'the only mass popular movement to affect critically the course of architecture in our century'.[4] The case of the McDonald's hamburger chain being forced into conserving an eighteenth-century vernacular house is a typical example of the American preservation movement's attempts to reverse insensitive built environmental decisions of the 1950s and 1960s. After McDonald's paid a million dollars for the site, they learned that they had to restore the building, which dated from 1795, to the condition visible in a 1926 photograph. Local residents had managed to designate the house as historic, and acquire protected status for it.

This case study, of Denton House in North Hempstead, New York State, also illustrates that large houses, like old factories and warehouses, are always prime candidates for conservation's best political, economic and design advice – that of 'adaptive use'. There is also the need for flexibility where new uses have to be considered to secure a historic building's survival. Adaptive use allows lateral thinking to achieve formerly unthinkable possibilities, such as another American example of converting concrete grain silos into a hotel. Robert Campbell wrote of the adaptation of buildings to new uses:

> Recyclings embody a paradox. They work best when the new work doesn't fit the old container too neatly. The slight misfit between old and new ... gives such places their special edge and drama ... The best buildings are not those that are cut, like a tailored suit, to fit only one set of functions, but rather those that are strong enough to retain their character as they accommodate different functions over time.[5]

In the United Kingdom it is only necessary to look as far as the latest television series of Channel Four's *Grand Designs* to see the invention, adventure and hard work, not to mention money, that people are prepared to put into adapting old buildings to new uses as dwellings. Some recent examples have included former water towers, electricity sub-stations, school houses, churches and chapels.

CRITERIA FOR CONSERVATION

Bernard Fielden suggests the following values for cultural property:

Emotional values: a) wonder; b) identity; c) continuity; d) spiritual and symbolic.

Cultural values: a) documentary; b) historic; c) archaeological, age and scarcity; d) aesthetic and symbolic; e) architectural; f) townscape, landscape and ecology; g) technological and scientific.

Use value: a) functional; b) economic; c) social; d) political and ethnic.

He goes on to say that 'Conservation must preserve and if possible enhance the messages and values of cultural property. These values help systematically to set overall priorities in deciding proposed interventions, as well as to establish the extent and nature of individual treatment.'[6]

Sir John Summerson suggests the following criteria for protecting historic buildings, which are quite similar to those mooted by Vanbrugh in 1709:

- The building which is a work of art: the product of a distinct and outstanding creative mind.
- The building which is not a distinct creation in this sense but possesses in a pronounced form the characteristic virtues of the school of design which produced it.
- The building which, of no great artistic merit, is either of significant antiquity or a composition of fragmentary beauties welded together in the course of time.
- The building which has been the scene of great events or the labours of great men.
- The building whose only virtue is that in a bleak tract of modernity it alone gives depth in time.

LISTED BUILDINGS

The Secretary of State for the Environment uses the following criteria when deciding which buildings to include in the statutory lists:

- **Architectural interest:** The lists are meant to include all buildings of importance to the nation for the interest of their architectural design, decoration and craftsmanship; also important examples of particular building types and techniques (for example, buildings displaying technological innovation or virtuosity) and significant plan forms.

- **Historic interest:** This includes buildings that illustrate important aspects of the nation's social, economic, cultural or military history.

- **Close historical associations:** With nationally important people or events.

- **Group value:** Especially where buildings comprise together an important architectural or historic unity, or a fine example of planning (for example squares, terraces or model villages).[7]

The age and rarity of a building usually denotes its historic importance, but obviously not necessarily its artistic or architectural interest – or lack of it. Consequently all buildings built before 1700 which survive in anything like their original condition are listed, while most buildings of about 1700 to 1840 are listed with some selection.

After 1840, the impact of the industrial revolution, and the consequent doubling in population over the course of the nineteenth century, predicated a vast increase in surviving buildings and ubiquitous building types. Greater selection is clearly needed so that buildings of definite quality and character are listed – for similar reasons only selected buildings after 1914 are normally listed. Buildings that are less than thirty years old are normally listed only if they are of outstanding quality and under threat.

Buildings less than ten years old are not listed. In the late 1980s William Waldegrave, then Environment Minister, added the 'ten-year rule' to the existing 'thirty-year rule', which enables buildings over ten years old to be considered for listing, providing they are of outstanding quality and in danger. The ruling was added because the rapid redevelopment taking place during the building boom of that era was threatening recently built heritage. Buildings are added to the statutory lists in two main ways:

1. As a result of systematic resurvey or review of particular areas or building types.
2. Following proposals from local authorities, amenity societies or other bodies or individuals that particular buildings should be added to the list ('spot listing').[8]

Ideally, listing *per se* is supposed to apply the statutory controls equally – but some buildings are more equal than others. When a building is listed it is graded, with Grades I and II* (two star) accounting for a small percentage (about 6 per cent) of all listed buildings that are of outstanding architectural or historic interest. Their significance to the national built heritage is generally beyond dispute. However, as Grade II buildings represent the other 90-odd per cent of listed buildings, which only 'warrant every effort being made' to conserve them, it follows that a building is 'safer', and surrounded by more restrictions on inter-

ventions, if placed in the relatively élite categories of Grade I or II*.

The present system evolved from such *causes célèbres* as the demolition of the listed Euston Arch in 1961 and the unlisted Firestone Factory in 1980. The specific grading of buildings varied between secular and ecclesiastic buildings until 1977. Anglican churches in use were graded A, B or C, and redundant Anglican churches were always notated in the secular manner. After 1977 the secular notation of Grades I, II*, II, and III was used for all building types. Grades I and II* represented about 6 per cent of all listed buildings. Grade III was a non-statutory grade that is no longer used: Grade III buildings were deemed to be of some interest, whilst not qualifying for the statutory list – though many of them are now being added to the list, particularly where they possess 'group value'. The hierarchy of listed buildings is now categorized as follows:

Grade I Of outstanding historic or architectural interest (11,600 buildings in 1994), in particular of great importance to the nation's built heritage; buildings of exceptional interest; of outstanding interest; of outstanding quality (approximately 50 per cent of buildings listed as Grade I are churches).

Grade II* Particularly important buildings in Grade II category (23,000 in 1994).

Grade II Of special architectural or historic interest, that warrant every effort being made to save them (approximately 94 per cent of listed buildings in 1994).

The grading of a building will affect the amount of grant funding available for its conservation, and the extent of legislative restrictions surrounding it. The 'list' is not just a long list of buildings in the entire country, but a collection of local lists, by local authority, parish, street and so on – including those of local importance because of their local history.[9] Buildings are usually listed by their curtilage, or site boundary – so that several listed buildings may occur within a single listed site or curtilage.

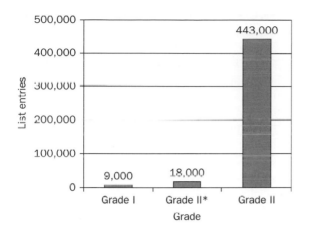

List entries by site for England, 1993.

Consequently the number of individual buildings will be correspondingly higher than the statistics cited for listed sites.

Grade II buildings are reviewed at a local level only, by local authorities, when listed building consents are applied for in conjunction with planning approvals for additions, alterations or, for that matter, demolition. Buildings graded above Grade II are considered by English Heritage in England, to ensure a considered review of important buildings by national experts.

The Scottish listing system is also classified into three categories: A, B and C. Category A is reserved for buildings of national or international significance. Category B listing signifies a building of regional, or more than local importance, or major examples of some period, style or building type which may have been altered. Category C implies a lesser example of Category B, or good groups of simple, traditional buildings. Similar procedures to the English system are administered by Historic Scotland, Cadw in Wales, and the Department of the Environment in Northern Ireland.

MAINTENANCE AND REPAIR

The key to the energy efficiency and the continuing sustainability of old houses is regular maintenance: it is the best and most economical way of conserving invaluable historic fabric, particularly in the case of listed houses. Dampness due to blocked up ventilation paths or rain penetration is the biggest threat to old houses. Clearly, a damp house will require more energy to heat it to habitable levels than a dry and well maintained one. Looking after a historic house is the day-to-day responsibility of owners and occupiers: just as we regularly service our cars on at least an annual basis, we should give the same consideration to our buildings.

A building that is well looked after will invariably retain its maximum value and avoid the need for extensive repairs due to failures caused by lack of maintenance. This is most crucial in the case of protection from water and damp penetration, such as damaged roofs, gutters, downpipes and the like. The chief cause of building failure is neglect, which can result in plants growing out of walls, overflowing gutters, and blocked ventilation grills. Maintenance is broadly divided into two main types: day-to-day actions of building owners and occupiers; and minor repairs carried out on an annual basis by a suitable builder and guided by appropriate specialist professionals.

Day-to-day maintenance involves such issues as clearing leaves and snow; controlling plant growth; looking for insect and fungal attack; removing bird droppings; and checking ventilation paths. Minor repairs and maintenance will include the following:

- minor works to slate and tile roofs;
- repair of existing leadwork and other metal coverings;
- refixing slipped lead and other metal flashings;
- maintenance of eaves' gutters and downpipes;
- maintenance of perimeter drainage channels or ground gutters;
- minor areas of mortar repointing to stone or brickwork;
- maintenance of external render;
- preventative treatment of timber against insect and fungal attack;
- minor repairs to small areas of internal plaster and associated redecoration;
- minor glazing repairs;
- regular painting of external woodwork.

Regular maintenance should minimize the need for major repairs to historic buildings. Maintenance inspections and a systematic regime focused on reducing the harmful effects of dampness on historic building fabric will delay the inevitable process of decay. However, some parts of the building will eventually reach the end of their life, such as roof coverings, windows and rainwater goods, for example. Preference must be given to replacing like with like, and continuing the legacy of traditional materials and vernacular building methods in a conservation area – otherwise the character, historic or architectural importance of individual buildings, and eventually the entire area, is lost for ever.[10]

When repairs are necessary it is important to discover and treat the causes of any defects and not just the symptoms, to avoid unnecessary damage, and to match existing materials and methods of construction. This strategy should conserve the appearance and historic integrity of buildings, and help to make sure that repairs have an appropriate life. The following principles are relevant to all historic buildings and provide a good starting point from which to understand the approach and philosophy to adopt in a conservation area:

- **Understand the purpose of repair or alteration:** The primary purpose of repair, or of any changes to old houses, must be to prevent or slow down the processes of decay without damaging their character, altering the features that give them their historic or architectural importance, or unnecessarily disturbing or destroying historic fabric.

- **Minimize intervention:** Interventions must be kept to the minimum necessary to meet the requirements of any appropriate use, within a structure that is sound enough to ensure long-term survival.

- **Avoid unnecessary damage:** The authenticity of a historic house depends crucially on its design and the integrity of its fabric. Unnecessary replacement of historic fabric, no matter how carefully done, will adversely affect the appearance of a house, seriously diminish its authenticity, and reduce its value as a source of historical information.

- **Seek reversibility, and minimize irreversible damage:** When carrying out alterations, always aim for solutions that can be reversed easily: therefore minimize vulnerability to irreversible damage, and plan new work so it can be removed, and the house revert to its former state, with minimum damage to the pre-existing fabric. This is particularly important when installing services such as heating and plumbing. The life of such services is usually very much less than that of the house as a whole. Short-term solutions for gains in comfort or efficiency should not put fabric that has survived, often for centuries, at unnecessary risk. 'Go round, don't cut through' is a good principle.

Most modern buildings are made of hard, strong and impervious materials; they rely on physical barriers such as damp-proof courses (dpc) and membranes (dpm), cavity walls and cladding to exclude moisture. Historic and traditional buildings are quite different, in that many have solid walls, and most have a porous fabric that both absorbs moisture and allows it to evaporate readily. This is often known as the ability of the building fabric to 'breathe'. To repair such buildings with modern materials is often inappropriate: for example, if soft sandstone walls are repointed with hard Portland cement and not soft lime mortar, not only will they look different and lose their attractive patina, but the new pointing may well cause the sandstone to weather badly. This leads to erosion and spalling of the stonework, while the hard cement remains. Such inappropriate repairs cause damage to historic fabric that has often survived for hundreds of years.

CASE STUDIES

Case Study 7.1
1930s Modern Movement house.

Key Points
- Refurbishment of a 1930s Modern Movement Grade II* listed building to its original appearance for family use.
- Upgrade to present standards of comfort and energy efficiency.
- Addition of internal dry-lining with insulation and vapour check to walls and roof.

- Addition of double glazing and low energy light bulbs.
- New electrical wiring and plumbing concealed within the internal dry-lining and insulation.
- Recipient of English Heritage financial grant aid for 50 per cent of the first stage of refurbishment.
- The occupants now regularly 'turn the thermostat down'.

General

This case study shows the successful rehabilitation of a Modern Movement house, with 100mm (4in) reinforced concrete walls, to present standards of comfort and energy efficiency. The story of 'Torilla', as the house is called, began with a chance meeting on the ski slopes of Switzerland in the winter of 1933–34. This resulted in the young English architect, F. R. S. Yorke's commission to design a modern house for a recently married couple. Yorke was only in his late twenties when he proposed the complex, well planned series of interlocking cuboid spaces. He used innovative forms of construction, such as flat roofs, *in situ* reinforced concrete and epically proportioned windows. However, the shock of the new also contains reassuring references to traditional English domestic architecture, such as the chimney stack and balcony – not to mention the eminently functional planning.

Torilla was listed and then de-listed in the 1980s, suffering three years of dereliction until pressure from conservationists in the 1990s resulted in its re-listing as Grade II*. Ultimately the house was restored by sympathetic owners with grant help from English Heritage, to a brief that reiterated the modernist aesthetic but with modern internal environmental comfort conditions.

Walls

The original walls of the house were 100mm (4in) thick reinforced concrete with an inner insulation lining of cork, although much of the latter had disappeared. This, and the generally derelict state of the house, actually made it easier to add an internal lining and insulation – as elaborate decorative finishes can mean aesthetic compromise when proposing dry-lining upgrades. All external walls were internally lined with 50mm of insulation and vapour check plasterboard, thinner around window reveals.

Windows

Most of the original windows were rusted solid and about half of them were replaced with new steel-framed, double-glazed sealed units. One single-glazed sliding door was completely conserved, and the other half of the window frames were retained but with added double-glazed sealed units.

Case Study 8.1 Modern Movement house refurbishment – entrance frontage.

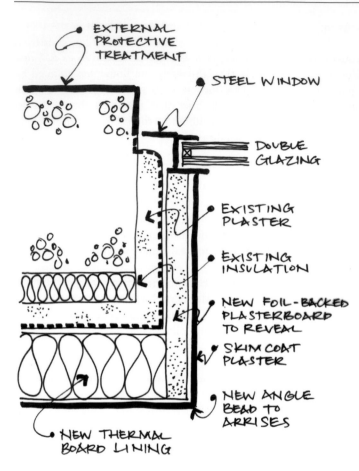

EXTERNAL PROTECTIVE TREATMENT

STEEL WINDOW

DOUBLE GLAZING

EXISTING PLASTER

EXISTING INSULATION

NEW FOIL-BACKED PLASTERBOARD TO REVEAL

SKIM COAT PLASTER

NEW ANGLE BEAD TO ARRISES

NEW THERMAL BOARD LINING

Case Study 8.1 Modern Movement house refurbishment – section through window jamb.

Roof

The underside of the ceiling was lined with 50mm (2in) thick insulation with vapour-check plasterboard.

Plumbing

The original plumbing was embedded in the structural concrete, and was badly rusted. New insulated plumbing was hidden within the new internal dry-lining and 50mm (2in) insulation layer.

Lighting

The original electrical wiring was run in conduits that were embedded in the structural concrete. The conduits were unusable, so new electric wiring was run in the new internal dry-lining and 50mm (2in) insulation layer. Some of the original 1930s light fittings were retained, and energy-efficient, long-life lamps were used where ceiling heights were too high for easy accessibility.

Note: A building does not have to be centuries old to be listed – some buildings as 'young' as ten years old are listed. There are many twentieth-century buildings that are listed, and they need to be approached in a way that reflects their formal protection. The Listed Buildings Act 1990 has provisions for fines up to £20,000 and six months imprisonment. Case law records fines of up to £75,000 for damage to listed buildings.

SUMMARY

- Five per cent of the UK housing stock is 'listed' or in designated conservation areas. This represents about 1¼ million dwellings, and about a quarter of all the buildings built before 1919. It is important to find out the status of any house in terms of protective legislation from the local planning office, before making too many plans for upgrading the building fabric, or starting any work on the house.

- It is a criminal offence to carry out, or to cause, unauthorized works to a listed building. The Listed Buildings Act 1990 has provisions for fines up to £20,000 and six months imprisonment. Case law currently records fines of up to £75,000 for such offences.

- The refurbishment of listed houses and houses in conservation areas is usually limited to measures that do not alter the appearance of the exterior of the house, and sometimes the interiors are also listed. However, there are still very many measures that can be taken to improve the energy efficiency and environmental sustainability of listed houses, such as increasing levels of insulation, secondary glazing to windows, and upgrading boilers, controls and lighting, without damaging legally protected historic fabric.

- Conservation is the action taken to prevent or slow down decay. In the case of historic buildings the object is to conserve the continuity of cultural and historic messages contained in the fabric and fittings. Minimal intervention on a reversible basis is invariably the best approach – such a philosophy does not prejudice possible future interventions, while avoiding fanciful reconstruction or 'restoration' on the basis of scant evidence.

- The foundations of historic building conservation are now enshrined in legislation. The Town and Country Planning Act (1944) took steps towards preservation on a scale more systematic and comprehensive than any country has proposed at any time. This Act was a response to the ribbon development of suburban houses sprawling into the countryside. Greenbelts were also established around towns and cities to avoid the development of continuous conurbations across the land. The pepperpot development of isolated rural houses was also targeted.

- The adaptive re-use of old buildings is the most economic form of conservation, as it finds new uses for often redundant building types. Television programmes such as Channel Four's *Grand Designs* show the invention, adventure and hard work, not to mention money, that people are prepared to put into adapting old buildings to new uses as dwellings. Some recent examples have included former water towers, electricity sub-stations, school houses, churches and chapels.

- The Secretary of State for the Environment uses the following criteria when deciding which buildings to include in the statutory lists: architectural interest; historical interest; close historical associations; and group value.

- The age and rarity of a building usually denotes its historic importance. All buildings built before 1700 which survive in anything like their original condition are listed, while most buildings of about 1700 to 1840 are listed with some selection. After 1840 the industrial revolution and population growth ensured the survival of ubiquitous building types, so that a more discerning selection of listed buildings is required – for similar reasons only selected buildings after 1914 are normally listed. Buildings less than thirty years old are normally listed only if they are of outstanding quality and under threat. Ten-year-old buildings can be listed if they merit it.

- Listed buildings are categorized in order of their importance, which reflects the level of legislative protection afforded to them. In England they are listed Grade I, Grade II* and Grade II; in Scotland they are listed as Category A, B and C; Wales and Northern Ireland have similar systems.

- Regular maintenance and repair are essential to ensure the energy efficiency and continuing sustainability of old houses. Dampness due to blocked-up ventilation paths or rain penetration is the biggest threat to old houses. Clearly, a damp house will require more energy to heat it to habitable levels than a dry and well maintained one. Maintenance is broadly divided into two main types: day-to-day actions of building owners and occupiers, and minor repairs carried out on an annual basis by a suitable builder and guided by appropriate specialist professionals.

- Principles for the conservation of listed houses include: understanding the purpose of repair or alteration; minimizing intervention; avoiding unnecessary damage; seeking reversibility; and minimizing irreversible damage.

CHAPTER 9

Renewable Energy

OVERVIEW

Renewable energy in old houses is hardly anything particularly new, as we have used renewable sources of energy, such as log fires, for centuries – millennia, even, if you include our time in caves back to the discovery of fire. In more recent times, the Roman architect and military engineer, Marco Polio Vitruvius, advocated orientating houses to the south to benefit from passive solar energy, particularly for the warming effect of the sun in the depths of winter. He even prescribed the displacement of rooms to take advantage of the path of the sun throughout the day, such as bedrooms and kitchens facing east to take advantage of the rising sun. And ultimately, most renewable energy comes from the sun: solar energy itself, tides and winds, and energy for vegetation to grow. Viewed in that way, the fossil fuels we are profligately burning now are the product of 'ancient sunlight'.

In medieval times, what we would call the lounge or sitting room was called the 'solar', which gives some clue as to the room's orientation – for daylight and warmth. These ancient, immutable principles obviously still hold true today and are used to design modern houses – some of which can also incorporate planning principles from historic houses, such as Edwardian butterfly-plan precedents (*see* Appendix E).

> The butterfly plan is predominately a nineteenth-century development, and characteristic of the Arts and Crafts Movement. It involves placing two or four wings of a house at angles to the core, usually at 45 or 60 degrees, to create a south-facing sun-trap.

The most obvious symbols of our dependence on the forces of nature for power, before the advent of electricity generation, are the remains of our industrial archaeology in the form of windmills and water wheels. Windmills had been used for milling corn and wheat into flour since medieval times, and many of them still dot our landscape to remind us of a former time without electricity at the flick of a switch.

Water wheels were also used for milling, and water mills also still occur in our countryside, although most of them no longer work, apart from a few for educational purposes – such as the Wellbrook Beetling Mill in County Tyrone, Northern Ireland (beetling was one of the final processes in the production of linen, and involved the water-driven powering of hammers to pound the cloth). However, they are an apt reminder of our need to site early industry in the most appropriate places, next to a source of renewable, clean and free power – not to mention the engineering feats required to slightly alter the courses of streams and rivers to take advantage of nature's bounty.

Now that we have gone through centuries of industrialization, during which we relied on the non-renewable burning of fossil fuels with their attendant pollution and carbon emissions leading to climate change, renewable technologies are reappearing in modern guise. Fortunately, most plans for industrial-scale wind or solar farms are necessarily sited in remote areas, such as out at sea or in deserts. However, there is an inherent conflict in the sense that remote areas on land tend to be in or near national parks and other places of natural beauty.

Conversely, an industry is developing in the provision of micro-wind turbines in urban and suburban

Windmill at Cromer, Hertfordshire, 1720.

Waterwheel, Wellbrook Beetling Mill, County Tyrone, Northern Ireland, 1760.

areas – although careful investigation into average wind speeds in specific locations is necessary to determine if payback periods are within the life expectancy of the turbine. Clearly, the location and height of the building will have a significant influence on the effectiveness of micro-wind turbines. There is a wide difference between locations for micro-wind turbines on houses, with payback periods measured in months for good locations, to circumstances where they never pay back.[1]

Solar water-heating panels achieved a degree of popularity during the energy crisis in the 1970s, and were fitted to many south-facing domestic roofs – mainly to pre-heat water. New technologies include evacuated solar tubes and photovoltaic solar panels that can generate electricity. However, careful calculations are required to assess the cost effectiveness of such investments, as new technology remains expensive, and there are usually more effective and basic

Wellbrook Beetling Mill, County Tyrone, Northern Ireland, 1760.

Micro wind turbines.

Edwardian house with solar tubes added to the roof.

places to start making old houses more energy efficient. The visible symbolism of renewable technology continues to hold a compelling sway over many of the most level-headed householders. It does at least ensure a clear conscience by the avoidance of some, if not all, dependence on central generation, with all its attendant disadvantages, such as transmission losses.

Renewable energy continues to remain part of the solution to our current energy and climate change crisis – as always.

Although many building conservation purists see conflict and contradiction in the application of modern technology to old houses, particularly listed houses, architectural aesthetics is a subjective area. In

Detail of solar tubes.

addition, many old houses contain more than one roof ridge with valley gutters, and these contain many south-facing roof slopes ripe for the application of 'hidden' solar panels. In the case of a listed farmhouse in the Peak District, an application to install solar heating panels was refused by High Peak Borough Council, but overturned on appeal. The Secretary of State supported the Inspector's view that as the existing roof tiles were as dark as the solar panels they would not detract from the character of the listed building, even though they were readily visible.[2]

As technology advances, already to the point where photovoltaic panels are made to fit individual roofing tiles, it is not difficult to imagine a time when any manner of colour, shape, texture or form of solar panels can blend seamlessly into the most treasured areas of our historic built environment – possibly saving

both them and us into the bargain. However, a suitable energy efficiency hierarchy is as follows:

- reduce the need for energy;
- use energy more efficiently;
- use renewable energy;
- make sure that any continued use of fossil fuels is clean and efficient.

SOLAR WATER HEATING

Solar water heating is a well known renewable energy technology in the UK, and can provide hot water at temperatures of 55–65°C (131–149°F). Typically, it can provide all hot water needs during summer, and about half of such needs all year round. Flat plate collectors are the cheapest and most common, but evacuated tubes and solar matting are also used. Domestic solar water-heating systems require solar collection panels or tubes, a heat transfer system and a hot water cylinder – the collection panels are usually fitted to the roof, facing between south-east and south-west. The typical retrofitted installation cost for a domestic plate collector of around 5sq m (54sq ft) is a few thousand pounds; evacuated tube systems tend to be slightly more expensive, but claim higher efficiencies.

SOLAR PHOTOVOLTAIC (PV)

Photovoltaic panels, or PV cells, convert sunlight directly into electricity. The solid-state semiconductors in the PV array convert the energy in light (photons) into electrical energy (volts), which gives them their name – photovoltaics. They come in a variety of colours, forms and sizes, down to individual roof tile sizes. They are usually roof mounted and are most effective in bright sunlight – an average domestic system of 1.5–2kW (peak) requires 10–15sq m (107–160sq ft) of south-facing roofspace. Typical installation costs are several thousand pounds, and a typical system should provide about half of an average family's electricity needs.

MICRO-WIND TURBINES

Micro-wind turbines for mounting on domestic roofs are an emerging technology, but their potential output is wide ranging and depends on the location and surrounding environment. Typical electrical output in domestic applications ranges from a few kilowatts to several, but can be less than 1kW. Although micro-wind turbines are designed to generate electricity from low wind speeds, a thorough assessment is necessary to determine the suitability of locations for installation. Typical domestic systems of up to 1kW cost a few thousand pounds, while large systems of several kilowatts will cost several thousand pounds.

Detail of photovoltaic solar panels.

HEAT PUMPS

Heat pumps move energy from one place to another and usually raise the temperature. A refrigerator is a common example of a heat pump. When heat pumps are used for heating, heat is taken from the ground, water or air and taken to where the heat is needed. The reverse process is used for cooling, with excess heating being dissipated into the ground, water or air.

A typical domestic system involves a series of underground pipes buried a few metres in the ground, or a borehole – water in the closed pipes is used to transfer heat from the ground to the heat pump within the house. Typical systems cost several thousand pounds, including the price of the distribution system. However, a ground source heat pump used for space heating is often cheaper than using oil, LPG or electric storage heaters, based on current fuel prices.

BIOMASS

Biomass is the term used for a wide variety of organic material, such as fast-growing trees (for example, willow and poplar for woodchips), waste and recycled wood, straw, and other waste organic matter. Biomass already represents the majority of the UK's renewable energy supply (about 1.5 per cent of UK primary energy supply).[3] Clearly, a suitable and reliable source of biomass fuel is required to consider this renewable energy option for domestic use – such as coppicing from a nearby forest. On a micro scale, a stand-alone wood-burning stove provides space heating for a room, and can be fitted with a back burner to give hot water. Central heating and hot water provision requires a larger system, with a boiler usually fuelled by logs, chips and wood pellets. Stand-alone room heating costs a few thousand pounds and running costs vary depending on the type of fuel used.

MICRO-COMBINED HEAT AND POWER (CHP)

Combined heat and power (CHP) uses the heat from the generation of electricity for space heating purposes, and is cost effective in building types such as hospitals, because they are continuously occupied with a consequent need for continuous space heating in the heating season. Micro-CHP units for domestic use are now available, and give each household the potential to become a mini-power station – also potentially eliminating the large transmission losses usually associated with supplying electricity from large power stations.

Micro-systems are usually powered by gas, and produce electricity and heat from the single fuel source. Many micro-CHP units are based on the Stirling external combustion engine (patented in 1816), which has a sealed system and uses an inert working fluid, such as helium or hydrogen. They are dissimilar to internal combustion engines and are no noisier than an ordinary boiler.

Domestic CHP units vary in size from half a kilowatt upwards, and currently cost a few thousand pounds. As electricity is only generated when there is a demand for heat, other supplies of electricity are usually required – unless linked to batteries or fuel cells to store electricity for use when the CHP unit is not running. Mass-produced CHP units should reduce in price in due course, and are worth considering when replacing boilers – payback periods of a few years are possible.

MICRO-HYDRO

Micro-hydro usually means electricity generation levels of less than 100kW, using naturally flowing water courses, such as rivers and streams. Clearly, unlike many other sources of renewable energy, micro-hydro is capable of continuous generation – in the absence of a drought. Energy demand is likely to be low when water flow is reduced in the summer. The scale of the potential micro-hydro scheme is dependent on the 'head' of water available (that is, the height of water that provides pressure to drive the turbine) and the water flow rate, which depends on the size of the watercourse and local rainfall. A typical domestic micro-hydro scheme costs several thousand pounds per kilowatt – £20,000 to £30,000 for a 5kW scheme. Economies of scale could result in a cost of a few thousand pounds per kW for larger schemes supplying a few hundred houses.

CASE STUDY

Case Study 9.1

Hydro-electricity in Cumbria.

Key Points

- Lake District hydro-electric scheme, originally installed a century ago but decommissioned in 1965, is reinstated.
- Residents set up their own power company – Coniston Hydro Electric Power.
- The new water turbine on Church Beck above Coniston supplies electricity for 300 homes in the village below, and is connected to the National Grid.
- Power is generated by using the water pressure to power a 15in (38cm) twin-jet impulse turbine, manufactured locally in Kendal.
- Demand for energy is highest in winter, when the beck is in full flow after heavy rainfall.
- Residents are now continuously happy, as they can enjoy both sunny days and heavy rainfall – for different reasons.

- Other sites throughout the Lake District are being considered for micro-hydro-electric schemes.

POSTSCRIPT

Once again the final words are best left to a recent government report on the existing housing stock in the context of climate change:

Modernization techniques based on air-tightness and ill-considered positioning of vapour barriers are often incompatible with property built traditionally, in which the ability of the fabric to move and breathe is vital for its long-term safety and future. A balance clearly needs to be found between the principles of conservation and carbon reduction. Former RIBA President, Jack Pringle, explored that balance in evidence to us: 'There are some houses, clearly listed buildings, that are so inefficient but so worth keeping that exceptions need to be made of them, and at the other end of the scale I am sure there are houses which are beyond hope, and it might be better to take

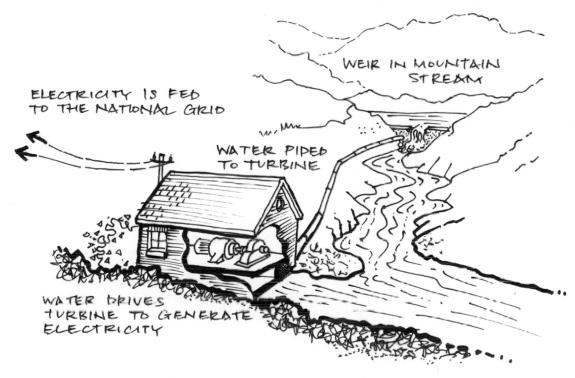

Case Study 9.1 Hydro-electric power in Cumbria.

them down and rebuild them, but I do not think they are in the forefront of our minds. We think that most of the building stock is susceptible to treatment.'[4]

[The report concludes that:]

We agree with Mr Pringle. The bulk of our housing, however old and leaky it may be, is capable of the kind of improvement that will deliver the necessary reduction in carbon emissions without destroying the visual character and appearance that makes it uniquely ours. We need neither a mass demolition programme followed by the construction of replacement eco-homes, nor to preserve every last pre-1919 building precisely as it was on the day it was built. The trick will be to find imaginative solutions as new markets and skills develop to bring new ideas and technologies to homes in which the 'low-hanging fruit' of draught exclusion and insulation has already been plucked.[5]

SUMMARY

- Renewable energy in old houses is not new, as we have used renewable sources of energy for millennia. Windmills have been used for milling corn and wheat into flour since medieval times. Water wheels were also used for milling and to power the nascent phase of the industrial revolution.
- Now that we have gone through centuries of industrialization, relying on the non-renewable burning of fossil fuels with their attendant pollution and carbon emissions leading to climate change, renewable technologies are reappearing in modern guise. Fortunately, most plans for industrial-scale wind or solar farms are necessarily sited in remote areas. Conversely, an industry is developing in the provision of micro-wind turbines in urban and suburban areas, but there is a wide difference between locations for micro-wind turbines on houses.
- Solar water-heating panels achieved a degree of popularity during the energy crisis in the 1970s. New technologies include evacuated solar tubes and photovoltaic solar panels that can generate electricity. Renewable energy continues to remain part of the solution to our current energy and climate change crisis – as always.

- The potential conflict of the application of new technology to old houses, particularly listed ones, could be resolved by the development of products, such as photovoltaic roof tiles, that blend seamlessly with our historic built environment.
- A suitable energy efficiency hierarchy is: reduce the need for energy; use energy more efficiently; use renewable energy; any continued use of fossil fuels should be clean and efficient.
- Solar water heating is a well known renewable energy technology in the UK, and can provide hot water at temperatures of 55–65°C (131–149°F). Typically, it can provide all hot water needs during summer and about half of such needs all year long. The typical retrofitted installation cost for a domestic plate collector of around 5sq m (54sq ft) is a few thousand pounds.
- Photovoltaic panels, or PV cells, convert sunlight directly into electricity. They are usually roof mounted and are most effective in bright sunlight – an average domestic system of 1.5–2kW (peak) requires 10–15sq m (107–160sq ft) of south-facing roofspace. Typical installation costs are several thousand pounds, and a typical system should provide about half of an average family's electricity needs.
- Micro-wind turbines for mounting on domestic roofs are an emerging technology, but potential output is wide ranging and depends on the location and surrounding. Typical domestic systems of up to 1kW cost a few thousand pounds.
- Heat pumps move energy from one place to another and raise the temperature. A refrigerator is an example of a heat pump. Typical domestic systems cost several thousand pounds. A ground-source heat pump used for space heating is often cheaper than using oil, LPG or electric storage heaters, based on current fuel prices.
- Biomass is the term used for a wide variety of organic material, such as fast-growing trees. Clearly, a suitable and reliable source of biomass fuel is required to consider this renewable energy option for domestic use. Central heating and hot water provision require a boiler usually fuelled by logs, chips and wood pellets. Stand-alone room heaters cost a few thousand pounds and running costs vary depending on the type of fuel used.

- Combined heat and power (CHP) uses the heat from the generation of electricity for space heating purposes. Micro-CHP units for domestic use are now available. Micro-systems are usually powered by gas, and produce electricity and heat from the singe fuel source. Domestic CHP units vary in size from half a kilowatt upwards, and currently cost a few thousand pounds. Mass-produced CHP units should reduce in price in due course, and are worth considering when replacing boilers – payback periods of a few years are possible.

- Micro-hydro usually means electricity generation levels of less than 100kW, using naturally flowing water courses such as rivers and streams. Energy demand is likely to be low when water flow is reduced in the summer. A typical domestic micro-hydro scheme costs several thousand pounds per kilowatt – £20,000 to £30,000 for a 5kW scheme. Economies of scale could result in a cost of a few thousand pounds per kW for larger schemes supplying a few hundred houses.

APPENDIX A

Glossary and Abbreviations

accreditation scheme All domestic energy assessors must be registered with an approved accreditation scheme in order to be able to register energy performance certificates.

acid rain Rain contaminated with sulphur and nitrogen in the atmosphere, largely caused by the burning of fossil fuels. The weak acidity of acid rain can corrode building materials such as limestone.

architrave An architectural decorative moulding of wood or plaster that derives from the classical orders of architecture, for example a ceiling or door architrave.

biomass Biomass is anything derived from plant or animal matter and includes agricultural, forestry wastes/residues and energy crops. It can be used for fuel directly by burning or after the extraction of combustible oils. Biomass heating involves the use of commercial energy crops in the form of fast-growing trees such as willow or poplar for woodchips, or waste wood products such as sawdust, pallets or untreated recycled wood for pellets. Stand-alone stoves provide space heating for a room, and can be fitted with a back burner to provide water heating. Boilers connected to a central heating and hot water system are larger and usually fuelled by logs, chips and pellets.

breather membrane A membrane that allows air and water vapour to pass through it, but which is impervious to water.

buttress Regular vertical and structural projections from a wall, intended to strengthen and support the wall against the horizontal forces that push out from the roof structure at the top of the wall.

Carbon Trust The Carbon Trust is an independent, not-for-profit company set up by the government with support from business to encourage and promote the development of low carbon technologies. Key to this aim is its support for UK businesses in reducing carbon emissions through funding, and supporting technological innovation, and by encouraging more efficient working practices. For further information visit www.carbontrust.co.uk

cavity wall Modern form of construction, generally appearing after about 1920, where two skins of masonry are built with a gap between them – originally connected with bricks or stones, then metal, stainless steel or plastic wall ties. The cavity was partially filled with insulation in new construction from about the 1980s.

CHP – combined heat and power A fuel-efficient energy technology that puts to use the by-product heat that is normally wasted. Micro-CHP is a small-scale and relevant technology for domestic use. It is likely to operate in place of a domestic central heating boiler, typically below 5kW electrical output.

classical Referring to the architecture of the ancient world, for example Greece and Italy.

classical orders The Greek and Roman architectural proportional rules for the arrangement of classical architecture into columns, capitals and entablature. The main orders are Roman, Corinthian, Ionic, Doric and Tuscan.

column A free-standing, vertical pillar. An 'engaged' column is attached to a wall; it is also known as a 'pilaster' when rectangular.

condensing boiler A boiler that contains a condenser to extract heat from the flue gases, and which causes water vapour in the flue gases to condense. Fuel and boiler efficiency is increased.

conservation area An area of special architectural or historic interest whose character and appearance it is desirable to preserve or enhance. Many nationally well known areas are designated conservation areas, and many of these comprise mainly housing, such as Bedford Park in London and Saltaire in Yorkshire. Conservation areas vary greatly in their nature and character. They range from the centres of our historic towns and cities, through to Georgian and Victorian suburbs and beyond. Conservation areas give wider protection than individual listed buildings, as the special character of these areas does not come from the quality of their buildings alone. The first conservation areas were created in 1967, and there are now over 8,000 in England.

Houses in a conservation area are part of the character and history that is being preserved. As planning controls will apply, seek advice from the local planning authority early in the process. Working with the local conservation officer and a specialist design consultant will ensure the correct path of action is followed.

conservation heating An environmental strategy employed by the National Trust to conserve the historic properties and contents in their custodianship. They rarely raise the indoor temperature more than about 5°C (10°F) above the temperature outdoors. This usually maintains a relative humidity (RH) in the range of 50–65 per cent, which is a good compromise for the conservation of most materials.

DEA – domestic energy assessor The name given to individuals who can produce EPCs for existing dwellings, other than home inspectors.

dew-point temperature The temperature at which water vapour in the air condenses to form condensation.

DPC – damp-proof course Impervious layer of polythene, bitumen or slate laid about 150mm (6in) above ground in the base of a masonry wall to prevent rising damp.

DPM – damp-proof membrane Impervious layer of polythene or bitumen usually laid under a concrete ground-floor slab to prevent rising damp.

drip-moulding or dripstone A simple or decorative moulding, often above a window or door, intended to direct water away from the face of the wall and the top of the window or door – to help prevent the weathering of the building fabric by avoiding excessive water penetration leading to dampness.

embodied energy Energy intrinsic to a material due to the effort that went into its extraction, processing, manufacture and transportation.

Energy Efficiency Advice Centres A network of centres across the UK providing free, impartial and locally relevant energy efficiency advice to householders and small businesses. Call free on 0800 512012.

EPC – energy performance certificate The mandatory energy efficiency assessment component of the HIP, compiled by DEAs and home inspectors.

EST – Energy Saving Trust The Energy Saving Trust is an independent, not-for-profit organization, set up and largely funded by the government and the major energy companies. Its purpose is to work through partnerships towards the sustainable and efficient use of energy in the domestic and small business sectors. To this end it manages a number of programmes to improve energy efficiency, particularly in the domestic sector. For further information visit www.energysavingtrust.org.uk

fuel cells A fuel cell uses hydrogen and oxygen (from air) in an electrochemical reaction. Unlike technologies that 'burn' fuel, with fuel cells the conversion takes place electrochemically without combustion. Fuel cells are used in portable applications (mobile phone and laptop battery replacements), mobile applications (cars, buses, planes) and stationary applications.

HCR – home condition report A voluntary part of the HIP.

heat pumps A heat pump moves heat energy from one place to another, and changes the temperature from lower to higher. An example of a commonly known heat pump is a domestic refrigerator. Where heat pumps are used for heating applications, heat is removed from the source (ambient air, water, soil or bedrock) and then discharged where the heat is needed. Where cooling is required, the reverse happens and heat is removed and discharged into air, water, soil or rock.

HECA – Home Energy Conservation Act Requires every UK local authority with housing responsibilities to prepare, publish and submit to the Secretary of State an energy conservation report identifying practicable and cost-effective measures to significantly improve the energy efficiency of all residential accommodation in their area; and to report on progress made in implementing the measures.

HIP – home information pack Since 14 December 2007 every home put on the market, no matter what size, must have a home information pack. The pack includes an energy performance certificate (EPC) containing advice on how to cut CO_2 emissions and fuel bills.

home inspector Licenced to produce full HCRs, which include an EPC. Home inspectors need to hold a diploma in home inspection, and be registered with a Home Inspector Certification Scheme.

hydro-electric power (micro-) Harnessing hydropower at micro-power level means levels typically less than 100kW, and involves utilizing naturally flowing water on land, usually rivers and streams. The type of turbine that is submerged into the water depends upon the site, the geological formation of the land and the flow of water present. The performance and size of micro-hydro schemes is very site specific, with plant ranging from a few hundred watts to 100kW, with the higher range used for commercial schemes.

infiltration Air entering a building accidentally and uncontrolled due to gaps and leaks in the building's fabric.

IPCC Intergovernmental Panel on Climate Change.

kW – kilowatt Unit of power (kW) equivalent to 1,000 watts or 1.34 horsepower.

kWh – kilowatt hour Unit of energy consumption (kWh) equivalent to using 1kW or energy for an hour.

Kyoto Protocol A protocol to the UN Framework Convention on Climate Change (UNFCCC) agreed in 1997. Developed nations are required to cut overall greenhouse gas emissions by an average of 5.2 per cent below 1990 levels over the period 2008 – 2012.

LED – Light-emitting diode Solid state light source that emits light or invisible infrared radiation when electricity is passed through it.

listed building The term 'listing' is used to describe a number of procedures used to protect our architectural heritage. When houses are listed they are placed on a statutory list of houses of 'special architectural or historic interest'. The older and rarer a house is, the more likely it is to be listed. Houses less than thirty years old are rarely listed, but an increasing number of post-war buildings is now being listed. In England and Wales, listed buildings are classified as:

Grade I – buildings of exceptional interest and national significance.
Grade II* – buildings of particular importance of more than special interest.
Grade II – buildings of special interest, warranting every effort to preserve them.

Scotland and Northern Ireland use similar classifications, labelled A, B and C. The local planning department (which may have a conservation officer) will determine the specific requirements for any work proposed to historic homes. The type of work requiring listed building consent varies with the building classification.

LNG – liquefied natural gas When natural gas is cooled to a temperature of approximately −160°C (−320°F) at atmospheric pressure it condenses to a liquid called liquefied natural gas (LNG). Natural gas is composed primarily of methane (typically, at least 90 per cent), but may also contain ethane, propane and heavier hydrocarbons.

low emissivity (low-E) glazing Glazing with a very thin metallic film on the side facing the building interior, which reflects some of the heat back into the room – improving the U-value of the glazing and leading to higher energy efficiency.

LPG – liquefied petroleum gas Usually propane or butane, derived from oil and put under pressure so that it is in liquid form. Often used to power portable cooking stoves or heaters, and to fuel some types of vehicle, for example some specially adapted road vehicles and forklift trucks.

MDF – medium density fibreboard Building material made of waste wood fibres compressed and glued into a rigid board.

NHER – National Home Energy Rating Scheme. The UK's first and largest quality-assured energy rating scheme – owned by National Energy Services.

night setback A feature of a room thermostat that allows a lower temperature to be maintained outside the period during which the normal room temperature is required.

NT – The National Trust A charity that relies for income on membership fees, donations and legacies, and revenue raised from commercial operations. They protect and open to the public over 300 historic houses and gardens and nearly fifty industrial monuments and mills. The NT also looks after forests, woods, fens, beaches, farmland, downs, moorland, islands, archaeological remains, castles, nature reserves and villages.

Palladian Classically inspired and symmetrical style of architecture configured by the Italian stonemason and Renaissance architect, Andrea Palladio – made popular in the British Isles by Lord Burlington and William Kent.

parapet The top of a wall that is taken above the roof eaves as part of the façade. Parapets are ubiquitous in Georgian houses, possibly originating from earlier defensive castellations and battlements. They can lead to water penetration and dampness unless well detailed and maintained.

payback period The period of time that has to elapse before the capital cost of an energy efficiency investment is repaid by savings. Simple payback is usually used, which does not take the future value of money into account.

pressure test Air pressure is tested in a building to determine the air-tightness of the building fabric. A fan blows air into a doorway and measures the volume of air delivered to maintain a given pressure.

prevailing wind The direction from which the wind usually blows – generally from the south-west in the British Isles. Cold and fast winds can also often come from the north or north-east.

PV – photovoltaics The direct conversion of solar radiation into electricity by the interaction of light with the electrons in a semi-conductor device or cell.

PVC – poly vinyl chloride

PVC-u – unplasticized PVC or **rigid PVC**

renewable energy Includes solar power, wind, wave and tide, and hydro-electricity. Solid renewable energy sources consist of energy crops, other biomass, wood, straw and waste, whereas gaseous renewables consist of landfill gas and sewage waste.

renewables obligation The obligation placed on licensed electricity suppliers to deliver a specified amount of their electricity from eligible renewable sources.

RH – relative humidity This is a measure of the quantity of moisture in the air, shown as a percentage of the maximum amount it could hold at the same temperature. Cold air can hold less moisture than warm air, so the RH in a room will increase as the temperature falls. An RH of 50–65 per cent is a good compromise for the conservation of most materials.

room thermostat A sensing device to measure the air temperature within a room and regulate the space heating. A single target temperature may be set by the user.

RSL – registered social landlords Non-profit-making bodies run by voluntary committees (RSLs) who provide rented accommodation at an affordable cost. Some also provide homes for sale through special schemes to help people on lower incomes become homeowners.

SAP rating – standard assessment procedure rating The energy performance of individual houses is measured using the government's standard assessment procedure (SAP), a rating scale of 1 to 100, in which 100 represents the best performance possible. SAP takes account of the fuel efficiency of heating systems and the thermal efficiency of the building fabric (that is, how well it retains heat in winter). It also takes account of other factors, including the type of construction (for example cavity wall, solid wall, terraced, semi-detached, detached or flat), the shape, size and orientation of the house, and the size and distribution of windows. A version of SAP, known as reduced data standard assessment procedure (rdSAP), is used to measure performance for energy performance certificate ratings.

SEDBUK – Seasonal Efficiency of Domestic Boilers in the UK An online database that contains performance data on over 3,000 boilers – www.sedbuk.com

solar photovoltaic (PV) electricity generation Generates electricity from sunlight. Small-scale modules are available as roof-mounted panels, roof tiles, and conservatory or atrium roof systems. The performance of a PV system will depend on the size of the system, the type of PV cell used and the nature of the installation. A typical domestic system may produce enough electricity to supply almost half an average family's annual supply.

solar thermal hot water heating The most commonly installed form of solar energy currently in use. It can typically provide almost all hot water requirements during the summer months, and about 50 per cent all year round. There are three main components for domestic hot water systems: solar panels, a heat transfer system, and a hot water cylinder. The solar panels, or collectors, are usually fitted to the roof and collect heat from the sun's radiation. This heat is used to raise the temperature of the household water and is delivered by the heat transfer system, which takes the heated water to the hot water cylinder for storage until use.

sustainability Sustainable development is progress that 'meets the needs of the present without compromising the ability of future generations to meet their own needs'. This is the Brundtland definition of sustainability.

temperature and time zone control A control scheme that makes it possible to select different temperatures at different times in two (or more) different zones.

thermal break An element of low conductivity placed within material of higher conductivity in order to reduce the rate of heat flow though the building element, such as a window frame.

thermal bridge A continuous element of building fabric that spans from the inside of the house to the outside and acts as a route for heat flow and loss, such as a continuous windowsill or lintel.

thermal mass Dense material, such as stone, concrete or brickwork, that can store heat. This accounts for the cool interiors, on hot sunny days, of thermally heavyweight buildings with thick stone walls, such as cathedrals. Thermal mass in houses can help to prevent excessive heat from solar gains in summer, but will generally take longer to heat up in winter than thermally lightweight houses.

thermostat An electronic device that measures temperature, and in the case of a house, maintains room temperature at a set point controlled by occupants.

thermostatic radiator valve A radiator valve with an air temperature sensor, used to control the heat output from the radiator by adjusting water flow.

time switch An electrical switch operated by a clock to control either space heating or hot water, or both together but not independently. The user chooses one or more 'on' periods, usually in a daily or weekly cycle.

trickle vent A small adjustable opening, usually placed in window frames, that allows building occupants to control background ventilation.

U-value A U-value is an indication of how much heat is conducted through a particular section of building construction. The lower the U-value, the better insulated the structure is. For example, a wall with a U-value of $1.0 \text{ W/m}^2\text{K}$ will lose heat twice as fast as a wall with a U-value of $0.5 \text{ W/m}^2\text{K}$. The rate of heat loss is measured in watts (W) per square metre (m^2) for every degree of temperature difference (K) between the inner and outer surfaces of the wall.

vernacular architecture Pragmatic construction, usually house building, in regional styles with local materials and craftsmanship – usually involving prosaic reactions to local weather, materials and customs.

weather compensator A device, or feature within a device, that adjusts the temperature of the water

GLOSSARY AND ABBREVIATIONS

circulating through the heating system according to the temperature measured outside the building.

wind turbines (micro-) These harness the wind to produce electrical power. The efficiency of a domestic system will depend on factors such as location and surrounding environment, and the electricity output is usually between 2.5 and 6kWs, but can be as low as 1kW. The latest development in domestic wind turbine technology is roof-mounted turbines for installation on domestic dwellings. These mini-wind turbines give a nominal output of 1kW and are designed to generate energy from low wind speeds. They are typically mounted on the gable end of buildings, although in some cases can be attached to the building side walls.

zone control A control scheme in which it is possible to select different times and/or temperatures in two (or more) different zones.

Further Reading

Anderson, W. (2007) *Green up! An A–Z of environmentally friendly home improvements.*

Barrett, H. and Phillips, J. (1987) *Suburban style: The British Home 1840–1960.*

Berry, S. (2007) *Fifty ways to save water and energy.*

Brand, S. (1994) *How buildings learn: What happens after they're built.*

Brereton, C. (1995) *The repair of historic buildings: Advice on principles and methods.*

BRE Trust (2006) *Sustainable refurbishment of Victorian housing: Guidance, assessment method and case studies* (FB 14).

Clift, J. and Cuthbert, A. (2006) *Energy, use less – save more: 100 energy saving tips for the home.*

Cumming, E. and Kaplan, W. (1995) *The arts and crafts movement.*

Department of Energy (1996) *Energy savings with home improvements: A practical DIY guide to improving your home and cutting your fuel bills.*

Dixon, R. and Muthesius, S. (1978) *Victorian architecture.*

Dow, K. and Downing, T. E. (2006) *The atlas of climate change: Mapping the world's greatest challenge.*

English Heritage (1994) *Draughtproofing and secondary glazing.*

English Heritage (2004) *Building regulations and historic buildings.*

Farris, J. (2005) *Ten minute energy saving secrets.*

Foley, G. (1987) *The energy question.*

Girouard, M. (1977) *Sweetness and light: The Queen Anne movement, 1860–1900.*

Gore, A. (2006) *An inconvenient truth: The planetary emergency of global warming and what we can do about it.*

Griffiths, N. (2007) *Eco-House manual.*

Harland, E. (2004) *Eco-Renovation: The ecological home improvement guide.*

Hillman, M. (2004) *How we can save the planet.*

Hollingsworth, A. (1987) *British building style recognition.*

Hughes, P. (1986) *The need for old buildings to breathe* (SPAB).

Hymers, P. (2006) *Converting to an eco-friendly home.*

Jackson, A. and Day, D. (2005) *Period house: how to repair, restore and care for your home.*

Johnson, A. (1984) *How to restore and improve your Victorian house.*

Johnson, A. (2006) *Understanding the Edwardian and Inter-war house.*

Laughton, C. (2006) *Tapping the sun: A guide to solar water heating.*

Lawrence, R. R. and Chris, T. (1996) *The period house; Style, detail and decoration, 1774–1914.*

Laws, A. (2003) *Understanding small period houses.*

Littler, J. and Thomas, R. (1984) *Design with energy: the conservation and use of energy in buildings.*

Long, H. (1993) *The Edwardian house: the middle class home in Britain, 1880–1914.*

Lovelock (2006) *The revenge of Gaia.*

Luxton, C. and Bevan, S. (2005) *Restored to glory: A guide to renovating your period home.*

Lynas, M. (2008) *Six degrees: Our future on a hotter planet.*

Mackay, D. J. C. (2008) *Sustainable energy without the hot air.*

Mazria, E. (1979) *The passive solar energy book.*

Morton, J. (1991) *Cheaper than Peabody: Local authority housing from 1890 to 1919.*

Muthesius, S. (1982) *The English terraced house.*

Naylor, G. (1971) *The Arts and Crafts movement.*

Oxley, R. (2003) *Survey and repair of traditional buildings: a sustainable approach.*

Pearson, D. (1989) *The natural house book: creating a healthy, harmonious and ecologically sound home.*

Pevsner, N. *The buildings of England, Scotland, Wales and Ireland series – various counties.*

Rock, I. A. (2007) *The 1930s house manual.*

Rock, I. A. (2007) *The Victorian house manual.*

Royal Commission on Environmental Pollution (1997) *Energy: The changing climate* (summary).

Saint, A. *et al* (1999) *London suburbs.*

Service, A. (1977) *Edwardian architecture.*

SPAB/IHBC (2002) *A stitch in time: Maintaining your property makes good sense and saves money.*

Thomas, A. R. *et al* (1992) *The control of damp in old buildings* (SPAB).

Van der Ryn, S. (1978) *The toilet papers: Recycling waste and conserving water.*

Waterfield, P. (2006) *The energy efficient home: A complete guide.*

Woolley, T. (2006) *Natural building: A guide to materials and techniques.*

ENERGY SAVING TRUST PUBLICATIONS

CE 16 (2003) *Cavity wall insulation in existing housing* (GPG 26).

CE 17 (2003) *Internal wall insulation in existing housing* (GPG 138).

CE 29 (2005) *Domestic heating by oil: boiler systems.*

CE 30 (2005) *Domestic heating by gas: boiler systems.*

CE 48 (2003) *Domestic central heating – systems with gas and oil-fired boilers* (GPG 284).

CE 49 (2003) *Domestic central heating – choice of fuel and system* (GPG 301).

CE 50 (2003) *Controls for domestic central heating.*

CE 51 (2005) *Central Heating System Specifications (CHeSS)* (GIL 59).

CE 52 (2006) *Domestic Condensing Boilers – the benefits and the myths* (GIL 74).

CE 57 (2004) *Refurbishing cavity-walled dwellings – a summary of best practice.*

CE 58 (2004) *Refurbishing dwellings with solid walls – a summary of best practice.*

CE 59 (2004) *Refurbishing timber-framed dwellings – a summary of best practice.*

CE 61 (2006) *Energy efficient lighting* (GPG199).

CE 83 (2004) *Energy efficient refurbishment of existing housing* (GPG 155).

CE 97 (2005) *Advanced insulation in housing refurbishment.*

CE 101 (2006) *Domestic energy efficiency primer – existing homes* (GPG 171).

GE 104 (2003) *Energy efficient refurbishment of existing housing – case studies.*

CE 118 (2006) *External insulation systems for walls of dwellings* (GPG 293).

CE 120 (2005) *Energy efficient loft extensions.*

CE 121 (2005) *Energy efficient garage conversions.*

CE 122 (2005) *Energy efficient domestic extensions.*

CE 124 (2006) *Energy efficient ventilation in housing* (GPG 268).

CE 137, CE 138 (2005) *Energy efficient historic homes – case studies.*

CE 184 (2006) *Practical refurbishment of solid-walled houses.*

CE 189 (2006) *Refurbishing dwellings – a summary of best practice.*

CE 193 (2006) *Refurbishment of non-traditional housing – case studies.*

CE 202 (2002) *Cavity wall insulation: unlocking the potential in existing dwellings* (GIL 23).

GPCS 318 (1996) *Energy efficient refurbishment of cavity-walled flats.*

GPG 175 (1995) *Energy efficient refurbishment of cavity-walled low rise houses.*

GPG 183 (1995) *Minimising thermal bridging when upgrading existing housing.*

GPG 294 (2002) *Refurbishment site guidance for solid-walled houses – ground floors.*

GPG 295 (2002) *Refurbishment site guidance for solid-walled houses – windows and doors.*

GPG 296 (2002) *Refurbishment site guidance for solid-walled houses – roofs.*

GPG 297 (2000) *Refurbishment site guidance for solid-walled houses – walls.*

APPENDIX C

Useful Contacts

Association for Environment-Conscious Buildings – www.aecb.net

Energy Saving Trust – www.est.org.uk

English Heritage – www.english-heritage.org.uk

Environment Agency – www.environment-agency.gov.uk

Cadw – www.cadw.wales.gov.uk

Environment & Heritage Service, Northern Ireland – www.ehsni.gov.uk

Georgian Group – www.georgiangroup.org.uk

Greenpeace – www.greenpeace.org.uk

Health and Safety Executive – www.hse.gov.uk

Historic Scotland – www.historic-scotland.gov.uk

Landmark Trust – www.landmarktrust.org.uk

National Inventory of Architectural Heritage, Ireland – www.buildingsofireland.ie

National Trust for Scotland – www.nts.org.uk

RIBA Register of Architects Accredited in Building Conservation – www.aabc-register.co.uk

Royal Incorporation of Architects in Scotland – www.rias.org.uk

Royal Institute of British Architects – www.riba.org

Royal Institute of Chartered Surveyors – www.rics.org.uk

SAVE Britain's Heritage – www.savebritainsheritage.org

SEDBUK – www.boilers.org.uk

Society for the Protection of Ancient Buildings – www.spab.org.uk

Sustainable Energy – www.withouthotair.com

Sustainable Energy Ireland (SEI) – www.sei.ie

Twentieth Century Society – www.c20society.org.uk

Vernacular Architecture Group – www.vag.org.uk

Victorian Society – www.victorian-society.org.uk

Top Twenty Tips

ENERGY EFFICIENCY

1. Only use the heat, light and appliances that you really need, and buy the most energy-efficient appliances. Consider metering all supplies.
2. If you have a thermostat, try turning it down by just 1°C (2°F), as this can reduce your heating bills by 10 per cent.
3. Insulate your hot water tank and hot water pipes.
4. Use energy-saving lightbulbs where appropriate (they use around a quarter of the electricity and last up to ten times longer than ordinary bulbs).
5. Make sure you have loft insulation that's at least 200mm (8in) thick.
6. Fit draughtproofing to windows and doors.
7. Improve your heating controls with timers, thermostats and thermostatic radiator valves (TRVs).
8. If you have unfilled cavity walls, and they are suitable, install cavity wall insulation.
9. If you have an old central heating boiler, fit a modern energy-efficient boiler when the boiler needs replacement. If you have old electric storage heaters, replace them with modern energy-efficient ones.
10. Install double glazing when windows need replacement and if appropriate – specify low emissivity double glazing. Install secondary glazing where appropriate.

ENVIRONMENTAL SUSTAINABILITY

11. Locally produced food and other supplies saves on transportation pollution.
12. Turn off lights and other electricity supplies when you are not using them. Electrical goods left on stand-by still use electricity.
13. Insulate your old house to save money and reduce carbon emissions. This and other cost-effective actions will help you to achieve a better rated energy certificate for your house.
14. Invest in white goods, such as fridges and washing machines, with A-rated energy use.
15. Public transport is more environmentally friendly than driving a car alone. H. G. Wells said: 'When I see an adult on a bicycle I have hope for the human race.'
16. Buy merchandise with minimal packaging. Packaging is energy intensive in its production, and wasteful if it cannot be recycled.
17. Reduce, reuse and recycle – glass, cans, paper and plastics. Give away old clothes and toys to support your local charity shops.
18. Write to your MP asking him or her to support measures to penalize the use of fossil fuels and give incentives to companies that use energy from renewable sources.
19. Use a water butt to collect rainwater for your garden and avoid using a hosepipe in hot weather.
20. Learn more about sustainability.

APPENDIX E

Butterfly-plan Sustainable House

Appendix E.1 Perspective view: butterfly-plan sustainable house. © M G Cook, RIBA, Architect.

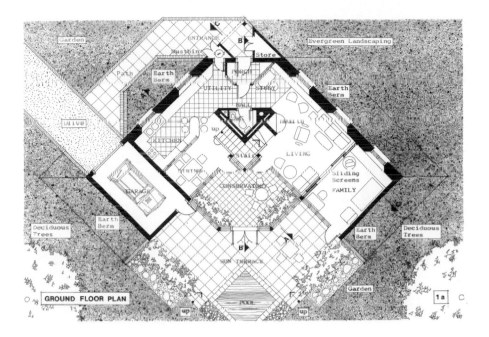

Appendix E.2 Ground floor plan: butterfly-plan sustainable house. © M G Cook, RIBA, Architect.

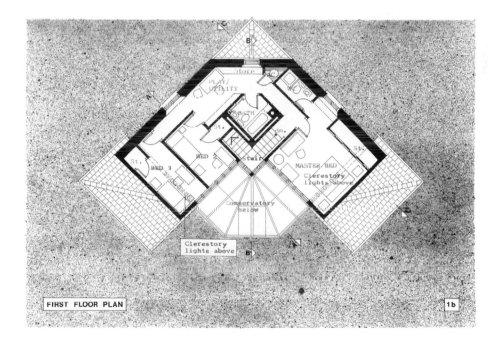

Appendix E.3 First floor plan: butterfly-plan sustainable house. © M G Cook, RIBA, Architect.

Appendix E.4 Section AA: butterfly-plan sustainable house. © M G Cook, RIBA, Architect.

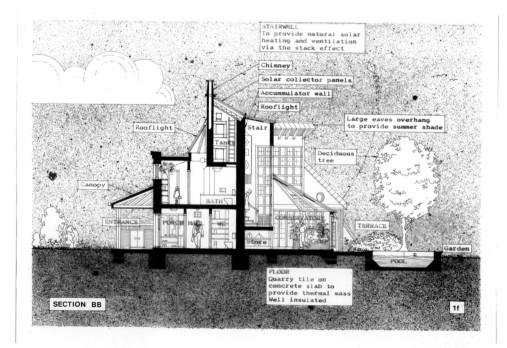

Appendix E.5 Section BB: butterfly-plan sustainable house. © M G Cook, RIBA, Architect.

References

Introduction
1 HM Treasury, *Stern Review on the economics of climate change*, 2006.
2 *The Daily Telegraph*, 31 December 2007.
3 J. Campbell, *Edward Heath: a biography*.

Chapter 1
1 B. MacArthur, ed., *Historic speeches*, 1995, Penguin.
2 S. Halliday, *The great stink of London*, 1999, Sutton.
3 M. Gaskell, *Building Control: National Legislation and the introduction of Local Bye-Laws in Victorian England*, 1983, Bedford Square Press.
4 William Lethaby, *Philip Webb and his work*, 1935, Oxford University Press.
5 Stefan Muthesius, *The English terraced house*, 1982, New Haven: Yale University Press.
6 A. Golland & R. Blake, eds, *Housing development: Theory, process and practice*, 2004, Routledge.
7 Nicholas Bullock, *Building the post-war world: Modern architecture and reconstruction in Britain*, 2002.
8 Peter Burberry, *Deteriorating design*, 1978.

Chapter 2
1 John Ruskin, *The seven lamps of architecture*, 1857.
2 H. Sandwith & J. Stainton, *The National Trust Manual of Housekeeping: A practical guide to the conservation of historic houses and their contents*, 2000.

Chapter 3
1 English Heritage, *Timber sash windows*, 1997.
2 The Georgian Group, *Windows: A brief guide to the history and replacement of windows in Georgian buildings*.

Chapter 4
1 Energy Saving Trust, *Practical refurbishment of solid-walled houses*, CE 184, 2006.

Chapter 5
1 George and Weedon Grossmith, *The diary of a nobody*, 1892.

2 Maureen Dillon, *Artificial sunshine: a social history of domestic lighting*, 2002, The National Trust.
3 Helen Long, *The Edwardian House: the middle-class home in Britain 1880–1914*, Manchester University Press.
4 Energy Saving Trust, *Domestic energy primer – an introduction to energy efficiency in existing homes*, CE101, 2006.
5 Energy Saving Trust, *Practical refurbishment of solid-walled houses*, CE184, 2006.
6 Energy Saving Trust, *Advanced insulation in housing refurbishment*, CE97, 2005.

Chapter 6
1 Finn Jensen, *The English semi-detached house*, 2007.
2 Energy Saving Trust, *Energy efficient refurbishment of non-traditional houses – case studies*, CE193, 2006.
3 Energy Saving Trust, *Cavity wall insulation in existing houses*, CE16, 2003.
4 Energy Saving Trust, *Minimising thermal bridging when upgrading existing housing*, GPG 183, 1995.

Chapter 7
1 Nicholas Bullock, *Building the post-war world: Modern architecture and reconstruction in Britain*, 2002.
2 Energy Saving Trust, *Domestic energy primer – an introduction to energy efficiency in existing homes*, CE101, 2006.
3 Energy Saving Trust, *Cavity wall insulation in existing houses*, CE16 (GPG 26), 2003.
4 David Pearson, *The natural house book: creating a healthy, harmonious and ecologically sound home*, 1989.
5 Energy Saving Trust, *Energy efficient ventilation in dwellings*, CE124 (GPG 268), 2006.
6 Energy Saving Trust, *Domestic condensing boilers – the benefits and the myths*, CE74 (GIL 74), 2006.
7 House of Commons, *Existing housing and climate change*, 2008.
8 House of Commons, *Existing housing and climate change*, 2008.

REFERENCES

Chapter 8

1 English Heritage, *The power of place*, 2000.
2 John Summerson, *Heavenly mansions, and other essays on architecture*, 1963.
3 R. W. Suggards and J. M. Hargreaves, *Listed buildings*, 1996.
4 Quoted in Stewart Brand, *How buildings learn: What happens after they're built*, 1994. Vincent Scully talking at the Charles Moore Gold Medal Presentation, 6 February 1991, at the National Buildings Museum, Washington DC.
5 Quoted in Stewart Brand, *How buildings learn: What happens after they're built*, 1994. R. Campbell and P. Vanderwarker (1992), *Cityscapes of Boston*, Houghton Mifflin, p.160–61.
6 Bernard Fielden, *Conservation of historic buildings*, Oxford, Butterworth.
7 Department of the Environment, *Planning Policy Guidance 15* (PPG 15), 1994.
8 Department of the Environment, *Planning Policy Guidance 15* (PPG 15), 1994.
9 R. W. Suggards and J. M. Hargreaves, *Listed buildings*, 1996, Sweet and Maxwell.
10 Christopher Brereton, *The repair of historic buildings: advice on principles and methods,* 1991, English Heritage.

Chapter 9

1 BRE Trust, *Micro-wind turbines in urban environments: an assessment,* 2007.
2 Roger Suggards and June Hargreaves, *Listed buildings*, 1996.
3 *Digest of UK energy statistics,* 2005.
4 House of Commons, *Existing housing and climate change*, 2008.
5 House of Commons, *Existing housing and climate change*, 2008.

Index